How to Catch a Shark

How to Catch a Shark

And Other Stories About Teaching and Learning

DONALD H. GRAVES

HEINEMANN
Portsmouth, NH

Heinemann
A division of Reed Elsevier Inc.
361 Hanover Street
Portsmouth, NH 03801-3912
http://www.heinemann.com

Offices and agents throughout the world

Library of Congress Cataloging-in-Publication Data

Graves, Donald H.
    How to catch a shark and other stories about teaching and learning / Donald H. Graves.
        p.   cm.
    ISBN 0-325-00027-1
    1. Education—United States—Biographical methods.
2. Teaching—United States—Anecdotes.   3. Learning—
Anecdotes.   4. Graves, Donald H.   5. Educators—United
States—Biography.   I. Title.
LB1029.B55G74   1998
370'.973—dc21   98-15736
                                                            CIP

Editor: Lois Bridges
Production: Melissa L. Inglis
Cover design: Judy Arisman
Manufacturing: Louise Richardson

Front cover photo: Don Graves and Bob McCarthy, Fairhaven, MA, 1949.

Back cover photo: Don and Betty Graves, Jackson, NH. © 1996 by Kucine Photography, Portland, ME.

Printed in the United States of America on acid-free paper
02 01 00 99 98   RRD   1 2 3 4 5

To my first teachers
Marion H. Graves
May 22, 1907–October 12, 1993
and
Wilfred (Hap) Graves
May 2, 1903–January 2, 1997

Contents

Contents

Acknowledgments

I am grateful to my first teachers, my mother and father, to whom this book is dedicated. They are no longer here but they continue to teach. About ten in the morning I hear Mother ask, "So far, what have you accomplished for the day?" I face a decision and I hear Dad say, "Do what you have to do that's right. Do what's professional." I am also grateful to my brother, George, whose quick judgment and love of sports and people has taught me much in growing up within our family and beyond. The people who demonstrate most in our lives are the people who teach us the most. Demonstrations last far longer than our words.

This book began nearly fifteen years ago. My first readers at that time were Mary Ellen Giacobbe and Donald Murray. Later, Jane Hansen and Camille Allen read various versions of the stories. Although my readers were always encouraging, I couldn't find a way to make the collection of learning stories into a book.

In September 1997, Mike Gibbons, Vice President and General Manager for Heinemann, told me he was about to observe some teaching by Mary Ellen Giacobbe in Lynn, Massachusetts. I said, "Well, I've got just the thing for you to read before you go." I hauled out "Independence," one of the pieces I'd written fourteen years ago about Mary Ellen's demonstration. I reread the piece and thought it still had relevance. I told Lois Bridges that I sensed there was a book but couldn't find the thread that would bind them together in a book. I mailed ten stories to Lois for comment. Lois saw more in the stories than I did and we decided they might be used to help others create their own teaching/learning stories.

Thanks go to our remarkable company, Heinemann, that

maintains the professional atmosphere so needed for teachers today. I have written and published with Heinemann for eighteen years. Mike Gibbons is lifting our professional visions still higher. His leadership allows me to create within an atmosphere of respect, so necessary for authors who want to take risks and push the edges of learning.

I am indebted to Lois Bridges for her fresh, insightful, and rapid responses. She knows how to be critical, yet maintains the vision for what the work can contribute to the profession. Thanks to her I couldn't wait to get to work in the morning. I took more risks in this book than I usually do because Lois was there with a strong safety net. That's precisely what good teachers have always done. Lois is the consummate teacher/editor.

My wife, Betty, has always been my first no-nonsense reader. She's also lived with me through many of the stories in this book. Betty is my continuing teacher, helping me to see more of the world than I could ever see alone. So many of the stories in this book began through something she first observed. In that sense she has been a coauthor for all my books. I am grateful for this partnership and can't wait to see where the writing will take us next.

The Power of Narrative

When I was six years old I told two stories that got me into trouble. The stories rolled off my tongue like water flowing downhill in a sweet April rain.

Dad had sent me to the store with a note asking for a can of Prince Albert, his favorite pipe tobacco. I enjoyed doing errands and chatting with Mrs. Bradley, the proprietor. She had white hair, pink cheeks, and kindly blue eyes, the sort of face you'd expect to find in a book of fairy tales. "What's new at your house, Donnie?" asked Mrs. Bradley.

"Well, Dad is going to work for the WPA."

"Is that so?" Mrs. Bradley replied with a touch of wonder in her voice.

"Yup. He's going to start Monday." Two days later Dad confronted me. "Where on earth did you come up with that story? I'm not going to work for the WPA and you shouldn't tell stories like that that aren't true." But I wanted the story to be true. About a week before, while riding the streetcar to the city, we passed a gang of men working on the highway with picks and shovels. They were stripped to the waist in the hot summer heat, digging in the dirt, and the sun caught their glistening, shimmering muscles.

Fascinated by the scene I asked Dad, "Who are those guys?"

"They are working for the WPA." The WPA stood for Works Progress Administration, an agency created by President Roosevelt for men who were unable to find work during the Great Depression of the 1930s. I liked the sound of the simple letters attached to strong, working muscles. Even though my dad had a job as a school principal, I wanted him to look as strong as those men working on the highway. The dream swirled around in my head for a few days until Mrs. Bradley's casual question released it, my first attempt at pure fiction.

Telling the story made it so. With a few words I could send Dad to work and bask in the glory of having adult news to tell. "He's going to start Monday." Don't people always start new jobs first thing Monday morning? I added that detail from stories I'd heard adults tell about people getting new jobs.

A week later I told Mrs. Bradley about going on a two-day boat trip with Dad. "Yes, we'll sleep on the boat overnight." Unfortunately, we didn't own a boat. Once again, Dad confronted me. I could tell he was embarrassed. "You can't go around telling these stories, because when people really need to believe you they won't pay attention. You aren't telling the truth." I guess Dad feared that my life was heading in sinister directions.

But to me, the stories were true because I needed them. I needed to do things that turned heads. I wanted Mrs. Bradley to think I was someone important. I cast myself as the main character and in the telling, I controlled the flow of events. Stories were my compass; they would guide me into a lifetime of adventure.

Why Story?

I meet a teacher at a workshop in Michigan. "You always lived here?" I ask.

"Not really. Moved out here about eight years ago. I used to live in a small town outside of New Bedford, Massachusetts."

"Which town? I used to live nearby."

"You wouldn't know the town. It's Mattapoisett."

"Good grief, my cousin lives there. Do you know her? Name's Field, Elizabeth Field." She used to work in a boatyard, and I discover that my new companion was an ardent sailor. Now that we've made a connection between our families, more stories will follow.

We live in a world that requires numbers: social security, credit card, bank account, hotel reservation, date of birth, passport, and driver's license. Young people are introduced to numbers that temporarily sum up their worth through their IOWA, PSAT, and SAT scores. We crave to be known beyond our numbers.

Just recently, I was asked to enlist in a direct deposit program for my social security check. I refused. Someone called me and asked a series of questions in a survey intended to cultivate my interest in direct deposit. When the survey was completed and my caller was about to hang up I said, "You know, you never asked me why I won't go for direct deposit. I realize the government doesn't really want to know, but I'll tell you anyway: I enjoy visiting with the tellers at the bank. We talk about the weather, their children, my writing, or how the garden is growing. We tell a story or two. I wouldn't miss that for anything."

Stories tell so much more of who we are. In an impersonal world we crave connection. Our stories tell about where we've been and where we want to go. As I tell my stories and listen to others, I reach back into my immediate and distant past and catch a bearing on where I am today. As I talk, I hear my words reaching toward where I want to go. Every story is an ontological event; it connects me with the universe. Some are large enough to reach back to my beginnings and to extend forward to my last days. They provide a foundation broad enough to encompass a world of living. I refer in particular to the story "Life and Death" later on in this book.

Life is always greater than we can express in mere words. For this reason, both children and adults naturally exaggerate when telling stories. Billy shouts, "The moose was ten feet high!"; his Dad speaks of the "great moose." "I caught a glimpse of him in the bog. I waited for what must have been nearly an hour until he finally ambled over to a tall stand of pine. The minute he hit dry land I got my close-up shot."

The philosopher Kierkegaard says that life is understood backwards but must be lived forwards. The medium of narrative allows us to understand the complexities of our lives by selecting essential elements that explain ourselves to ourselves. My story about an incident in the past provides a platform on which I can stand, then step with greater confidence into the future.

STORIES AND THE PROFESSIONAL LIFE

Stories are an essential part of my life as a professional. "There was this child who . . . Let me tell you about the time I tried to teach some grammar; I can't believe I did it that way but I've been watching the way my daughter taught her niece how to set the table. She made a story out of it . . . and it works . . . I've got a headache; just got out of our curriculum meeting and we've been outflanked by the testing department. You'll need to sit down to listen to this one. . . ."

Robert Frost spoke of poetry as a momentary stay against confusion. I would submit that stories do the same. Stories reach for the essential elements. They reintroduce the human into our profession, which is also afflicted by the world's growing impersonality. Teachers everywhere try to teach in an era of ever-escalating pressure, inflating curriculum, and ceaseless classroom interruptions. Our best professional efforts are often measured only by the numerical scores our children achieve. I have no quarrel with achievement tests, but when they are used as the sole currency for explaining human growth, I hit the ceiling. I believe that the well-chosen, well-told, story can tell more about the qualitative status of both teaching and learning in the classroom.

Classroom Stories
We need to be articulate about our best and our worst teaching moments. Sometimes I make a list of both, and I find it important to attach the names of specific children or teachers.

I've told the story of Brian Ashley dozens of times to myself and to audiences across the country. Brian was a fifth-grade student who was several reading grade levels below the other children. Worse, he scarcely read on his own. Brian was able to become a reader through his love of nineteenth-century whaling. He was a participant in a program that invited children to focus on an aspect of learning of interest to them. At first Brian read pictures, then captions to go with the pictures. He switched to information books prepared for primary children, gradually built up his vocabulary, and soon moved on to more difficult books.

Brian constructed whaling ships and models of various types of whales out of papier-mâché. When he gave his report to several classes, he reenacted a whale chase with ship and whale on top of two long tables. At the end of the presentation, children fielded questions from the audience. One boy asked, "Brian, did a whale ever sink a ship?" Brian wrinkled his face, paced a moment with his thumbs tucked into his belt like a university academic, and then replied, "Yes, the cutter

Essex out of Nantucket was sunk by a large sperm whale off the coast of Chile in 1820. The whale may well have been Mobius Dick, made famous by Herman Melville, who changed the name to Moby Dick. Next question." The audience gasped. They were amazed that the Brian they knew was spouting such knowledge.

Brian put all his time into studying whales, to the neglect of other aspects of the curriculum. Strangely, however, his grades went up in other subjects: he had not only fallen in love with whaling, he had learned how to learn. I use this story to show how important it is for children to fall in love with some area of learning.

I also have stories that are not so pleasant. David, for example, was a grasshopper of a kid. Small of stature, he was an itch that made everyone want to scratch. Four seconds after he walked into a room the noise level would go up two decibels. His hands had to poke, punch, or engage in some manner of contact that caused a commotion. He knew all my buttons and pressed them at will. Late one Friday afternoon, when my patience matched the falling barometer, David touched off an argument in the corner of the room. When I walked over, David produced his usual "I didn't do nothin' " demeanor. I caught him near the chalkboard, grabbed his shirt beneath his chin, and lifted him slightly, at the same time twisting the shirt. Only the terror in his eyes made me stop. When the last bus had departed I sat at my desk shaking with remorse over what I had nearly done. On Monday morning I pulled David aside and told him how sorry I was about what had happened. We began to discuss our difficulties, and I followed up with a trip to his home. Things improved, but that awful moment has served as a warning to me that the possibility of violence is ever at hand.

I haven't told David's story to large audiences; indeed, this is the first time I've admitted that such an incident ever occurred. Yet it was important for me to write it down to try to understand one of the darker moments in my teaching career. Why was it so important? The incident occurred during my second year of teaching, when my repertoire for both understanding and teaching was rather limited. Certainly my compassion for teachers who "cross the line" is greater now. I suspect that my exasperation at David's intransigence and my own ineptness reached a blowup point. I simply didn't know how to mediate my feelings more gradually. I needed to share these stories with colleagues, but I felt so inadequate as a teacher that it was hard to admit my failure. If I had been able to tell stories about my Brians, perhaps that would have helped me to tell about my Davids.

Teaching/Learning Stories

From the time we get up in the morning until we retire in the evening, we are surrounded by teaching/learning events. Thousands of stories become part of us during our lifetime. The question is, can we recall these stories with any profit? Can I reach back and recall stories that might help me not only to understand myself but to assist others in teaching and learning? Twelve years ago I set out on an expedition. I began by making lists. I listed everything I knew how to do: tie my shoe, drive an automobile, mow the lawn, read, write, row or scull a boat, shave, take photos, save money, or hybridize gladiolus. I then tried to recall the persons involved in my learning, and that usually helped me to recall the actual teaching/learning event. Of course there were many skills for which I simply had no memory of either a teacher or a learning event, but enough remained to begin to structure a range of significant stories that allowed me to see teaching and learning in a different light.

I began to write out each of these learning stories and found that rapid writing was a great aid to memory. I lowered my standards, blasted away on the text, and changed little until I got to the end and went back to revise. Writing was itself an act of memory. I'd begin with only a vague memory of the teaching/learning event and end with a fully fleshed out story.

One story led to another. So many of my views about teaching and learning, I realized, came from the demonstrations and homilies of my mother and my father, my first teachers. My concepts of time and space, justice, ethnic identity, health, birth, life, death were established by my parents. My notions about growing up came from relatives I saw only once or twice a year. Much of my learning was the result of observing adults in the process of doing things: Grandpa cooking, driving a car, or doing light carpentry; Uncle Nelson sculling a boat or building a stone wall.

My teaching sense was born of a village of teachers—my family, those in public school and university, and others I encountered even briefly. Later, married with five children, I continued to learn as I tried to teach within the family.

I was twenty-six years old when I first began to teach. Just out of four years in the U.S. Coast Guard, I was assigned to thirty-nine seventh graders in a grade one to seven rural school. Worse, I began after only an eight-week teacher preparation course. A national shortage of teachers in 1956 led to desperate measures to attract people to the profession and then prepare them for immediate arrival in the classroom. I floundered. I was so anxious before school, I couldn't eat breakfast for the first nine months.

My stories saved me. I drew on every bit of teaching and learning lore I could recall. I told stories in class and worked hard to release the stories of my students. Somehow we all survived intact until June.

A common dictum in both teaching and writing is "show don't tell." Good teaching is more showing than telling. I use math manipulatives or compose a text on the overhead projector, but I also illustrate human learning and experience through stories: "Let me tell you about the time when I learned how to hold a twelve-foot boa constrictor" or "The other day I saw Philip's team figure out a new way to get resources for their project. Tell us how you did that, Philip."

No story is a story unless the main character wants something and wants it badly, says the playwright Neil Simon, and every story reflects learning. The main character sets out on a journey to realize a want or a wish and encounters difficulties because the force of the wish is substantial enough to create waves. The journey bends toward a conclusion and for better or worse the main character learns. What follows is a collection of stories gathered over a lifetime, some sixty years old, others only a few weeks. As you read my stories, my fondest wish is that you will say, "Yes, that's true, but listen to what happened to me." It will be your turn to tell yourself a story and then share it with others.

Breakfast

One of my earliest recollections is tumbling into my parents' bed-room in the early light of dawn and asking for something to eat. My father never moved from sleep but Mother replied, "For heaven's sake go back to bed; it's only five-thirty in the morning."

I didn't go back to bed. I was wide awake and wanted to play. I'd get out my trucks or construct a tent out of a card table and blankets. Sometimes, if I needed a play companion, I'd wake up George, my younger brother.

The only hazard to waking up early was hunger. I woke with an empty tank and an engine that needed fuel. Before I was six I'd stick out the hunger and play until Mother got up at about six forty-five. I remember the headaches that accompanied an empty stomach but also the relief of breakfast.

Mother didn't have to sell me on the virtues of a good breakfast, but she did anyway. Getting a jump start in the day was important to her. Even though her mother lived 250 miles away, she could still hear her voice: "Marion, it's ten o'clock in the morning; what have you accomplished for the day?" A fast start meant beginning with the right food, and breakfast was the foundation, the reason why people got ahead, the mark of the virtuous life.

The centerpiece of Mother's breakfast was hot cereal. Occasionally we'd have a boiled egg, but steaming hot cereal was her hallmark: oatmeal, cream of wheat, Ralston, Petty John, or Maltex with sugar and milk, supplemented by orange juice, milk, and toast. "Got to have something that will stick to your ribs. Those other breakfasts won't last past ten o'clock."

The "other" breakfasts—cold cereal, sweet rolls, or English muffins—were damned. Mother seldom lectured about food, but there was no mistaking the morality of hot cereal.

I wondered about Wheaties. On the back of the box my

hero, Ted Williams, touted the power of the Breakfast of Champions as he lifted another home run into the right field bleachers at Fenway Park. "Mom, Ted Williams says eating Wheaties helps him hit home runs. How come we don't eat Wheaties?" George and I dreamed of playing for the Red Sox.

Mother would hear none of my arguments. "Yes, and what does Ted Williams accomplish by ten o'clock in the morning?" Well, I didn't know what Ted Williams did in the morning. He only played ball in the afternoon, so I had nothing to say.

On one occasion Mother had to go to Massachusetts to take care of her sick grandfather. She was a nurse and often got called on by sick relatives to help out. Dad took care of breakfast as best he could, but he didn't know how to cook and was scarcely able to boil water. He bought some Wheaties. I ate them with gusto, imagining that their power was reaching out to my biceps. That day I went to school ready to hit home runs at recess.

I remember watching the clock. When nine forty-five rolled around in the midst of mathematics, I began to feel a slight panic. I began to feel the power of Mother's lectures. "And what will you be able to do by ten o'clock?" I tried a row of math examples. Suddenly I couldn't add. Nothing made sense. I could hear Mother from 250 miles away, "What does Ted Williams know?"

Our parents often have particular views about food that come to occupy a moral center in our lives. Mother grew up on a farm where breakfast was very important. The farmhands would start their chores between four-thirty and five and be ravenous by seven. Hot cereal was at the heart of a good day.

Work and food went hand in hand along with predictable times for eating. Even though we lived in the city, mother still maintained farm routines: breakfast at seven, lunch at noon, supper at six. Midmorning was the first checkpoint for evaluating work thus far accomplished. "It's ten o'clock, Marion, what have you done?" I still hear Mother's voice asking the same question today.

TRY THIS: Consider any routines your parents established in your life as you grew up and particular foods they felt important to your well-being. Try to recall an event or a story that exemplifies their views.

Shoe Tying

"Donald, any five-year-old ought to know how to tie his shoe," proclaimed my mother. Mother, a self-reliant New England native, wanted the same independence for her children. Learning to tie my shoe is my first recollection of learning to do anything.

Mother motioned me toward the six-foot couch that was the centerpiece of our meager depression-era furniture. The couch arm was open underneath except for two struts, each about as high as my chest and just below eye level, that connected it with the main structure.

"Be back in a minute." She returned with the thick tie from her bathrobe. "Now watch," said Mother, "there's nothing to it." At near eye level I was able to watch every step. With grace and confidence she brought the tie under the arm of the couch. Then, she took the two ends of the tie, crossed them, looped one under the other and pulled it taut. "Now you try it."

I hesitated. "Pick up the two ends." She took my hands in hers. "Now cross, pass this one under the other, and pull. There, it's easy isn't it? Go ahead and try it yourself."

Under her confident gaze I crossed the two ends, looped one under the other, and pulled them taut. I'm not sure which felt better, my new independence or living up to Mother's expectations. Then she proceeded to show me how to make loops, a much more difficult enterprise. By now I was sure she could show me how to do almost anything and I would be able to do it.

Tying the thin laces of my own shoes at floor level was still difficult, but Mother had already established the fact that I was a learner. She adjusted the learning field to eye level, enlarged the size of the materials by using the thicker tie from her bathrobe, and demonstrated how it was done. Dad was a school principal and educator, but Mother, a registered nurse with a Yankee notion of how to simplify complex aspects of living, was my most important and immediate teacher.

This is my first memory of learning how to do something. I knew my mother was a good teacher, but when I analyzed how she taught me, I realized how well she structured my learning.

Our parents are often our first teachers. The way we are taught as children shapes the way we pass that learning on. Indeed, these experiences are our first preparation as well as our first instruction in showing others how to do things, whether we go into a teaching career or not. For better or worse, everyone is a teacher.

TRY THIS: Recall an early teaching experience with one of your parents. Recapture the details. How do you think their teaching in that episode or in other kinds of instruction have influenced you as a teacher? Discuss.

Life and Death

I wrote this story in the first person and the present tense to represent the situation as it happened to me when I was a child.

Mother is pregnant and happy about it. Sometimes she lies down on the couch and calls us over to feel the baby kick. "Put your hand right here, George," she says. "Feel him?"

I press in closer. "I want a turn. I want to feel the baby kick." I feel a little tremor against my hand. Although Mother is bigger around the middle, I can't quite believe there's a baby inside. "How does the baby breathe in there?" I ask. I have lots more questions.

"He doesn't really breathe and eat the same way you do, but there's a tube inside me that goes to the baby; it's pretty complicated. I'll try to draw it out for you on a piece of paper tomorrow." I picture a tube like those I've seen go into men's deep-sea diving helmets, only air and meat and potatoes go down through the line to the baby.

"If it's a boy, we'll name him John and if it's a girl we'll name her Jean," Mother says. We like the names but we want another brother.

"Which do you want, Mom, a boy or a girl?"

"I don't really care. All I want is a healthy baby. That's the important thing."

Mother wants us to know where babies come from. She doesn't agree with Grandma Hiller who thinks it's a mistake to let children know such things. Mother doesn't care. She's a nurse and she'll tell us almost anything we want to know. She likes it when we ask questions.

"I'm telling you about where babies come from because you are *my* sons. So keep it to yourself until you get older. Not all the other kids' mothers will appreciate the fact that I'm telling you all about babies. Besides, it's their business whether or not they want their sons to know." I feel smart because I know about babies and how they breathe and get food inside their mothers.

Mother hires a young Negro woman, Clara, to help with the housecleaning. We can't afford it, but Dad won't have it any other way. He wants Mother to take it easy and not work so hard. I don't know any Negroes because none live near our street. I already know from Mother's reading of history books that Lincoln freed the slaves who were Negroes.

When Clara works I follow her around the house. I like to look at her. She looks warm and smooth and her voice is deep. When she sings I hear lovely music I've never heard before. When I follow her the questions grow inside me. "Were you ever a slave?"

Clara laughs, "Oh my heavens, no, but my great grandfather was a slave, but not me." When Clara works she sings in a deep, mellow voice. She listens patiently to my many questions: "Do you like to sing? Is this hard work? Do you have brothers and sisters?" One day she stops what she's doing and asks, "Where do you get all those questions, boy?" She laughs as she speaks, shakes her head and goes back to work.

I can't ask enough questions. I want to be near her, listen to her talk. Clara has smooth skin I want to touch. One day I stand next to her when she's drinking coffee at the kitchen table and I put my hand on her arm. It feels warm and comfortable. I think she's the most beautiful woman I've ever seen. Smiles, song, and smooth skin are connected to cocoa color in my mind. She only comes one day a week during the last months of Mother's pregnancy.

George and I keep asking Mother, "Is it time yet? When will the baby come?"

"Soon enough," Mother says with a smile. "Soon enough." But we can tell she wants it to come real soon. She's excited about the baby like we are.

Early one morning I hear Mother cry from her bedroom, "Oh Hap, I'm bleeding. Oh no. Call the hospital ambulance quick!" After that I can hear her crying, "Oh my God, no!"

George and I jump out of bed to see what the trouble is. Dad is already on the phone. "Don't go in to your mother," he says, standing there in his underwear. His face looks worried and sad, like the time he told us Uncle Hal and Grampa Sanderson died in the fire.

In a few minutes we hear a siren. I run to the front window and there's an ambulance and two policemen taking a stretcher out of the back. The ambulance looks like the same truck that delivers our milk. The policemen come right in the house and in minutes they are carrying Mother around corners in the house on a stretcher. Everyone is in a hurry. Mother is covered in blankets up to her chin. Her face looks sad and she's crying when she goes by us on the front steps. "Don't worry boys, it'll be all right."

She doesn't sound very sure. Dad climbs into the back of the ambulance with the policemen and the ambulance roars away, the siren waking up everyone in the neighborhood. People come out to their front stoops in pajamas and bathrobes to see what's going on.

Mrs. Pym, our landlord, is with us in her bathrobe when the ambulance takes off with Mom and Dad. She says, "We must bow our heads and say a prayer for Mother and the baby." She sounds very serious. "Lord Jesus, protect Mother and the baby. We know you love them. We ask this in the name of our Lord and Savior, Jesus Christ. Amen."

"Will God protect them? Really?" I ask Mrs. Pym.

"Oh yes, if you ask in the name of Jesus, He will," Mrs. Pym says. "Oh yes, He will. Can you boys get yourselves dressed all by yourself so I can get us some breakfast?" We assure her we can.

All that day I keep looking out the window to see if Mom and Dad are coming back. Mrs. Pym says calmly, "It's all right. I know everything is all right."

George asks, "Is she having the baby now?" He doesn't seem worried like I am. In fact, he sounds excited.

"I don't know. I'm sure we'll hear something soon."

We eat breakfast, lunch, and supper with Mrs. Pym. It is dark. Just before it is time to go to bed, Dad comes in the front door. We race to meet him. He looks tired and he's shaking his head. "I think Mother's going to be all right," he says softly. "It was nip and tuck there; I was afraid we'd lose her. We did lose the baby though. They couldn't save him. It was a boy, a nice big boy. They showed him to me. He never had a chance because the cord that fed him came off too soon and that's why Mother was bleeding so much."

I shout, "God can't do this to us. We even prayed!" Mrs. Pym seemed so sure, and she goes to church every Sunday and reads the Bible.

George begins to cry, "The baby's dead?" Now he's angry, "Why couldn't they save the baby?" Dad doesn't know what to say. He sits down in his big chair. "Boys, we almost lost Mother but she's going to be all right." Dad can't talk about the baby; he's so glad he still has Mother. Neither George nor I can believe that our mother could die.

"I've called Grandma Sanderson. She'll be coming in on the train tomorrow at noon at Grand Central Station. I'll go get her. She'll be here for the first week. Grandma Hiller said she'd come the second week. Mrs. Pym said she'd help out until tomorrow afternoon. Now you boys get yourselves ready for bed. I've got to get on the phone and make some more calls. Then I'm going back in to see Mother."

George is crying, "The baby's dead. Why is the baby dead?"

I'm supposed to be big brother but I'm crying too. I want to talk with Mother so badly. I want her home right now to explain things, to see if she's all right.

I get up the next morning feeling tired and not wanting to go to school. I miss the sounds of Mother bustling in the kitchen, the smell of oatmeal cooking in the double boiler. This morning there is no orange juice set on the table. My yellow cereal bowl with the brown doggie on the outside is not next to my napkin folded inside the ring that holds it in place.

I can hear Dad in the bathroom. I walk toward the bathroom and find him shaving at the sink. "When is Mom coming home? I want Mother. I want to talk to her," I say, my voice rising with each phrase.

Dad taps his razor in the bowl and turns his head still half-lathered in white soap. "Mother is very sick and she won't be home for quite a long time, but Grandma Sanderson will be here this afternoon. I'm picking her up around noon today. She's coming as fast as she can."

"I don't want her. I want Mother!" I shout. "And I'm not going to school either." I feel the tears filling my eyes. I'm mad and I want Dad to know it.

"I'll talk to you in a minute. Just let me finish this." He speeds up the shaving, pulling the razor up his neck toward his chin. "Oops," he says and I see he's cut himself. The blood flows bright red through the white shaving cream. I'm glad he's bleeding. I want him to hurt. I want Mother.

Dad sticks a piece of toilet paper on his neck to stop the bleeding, then turns to me trying to sound calm. "Now go into your bedroom and get dressed. Try and help George. I need lots of help today. I've got to get to school, get Grandma, and see Mother."

I feel a little better after yelling at Dad and seeing him bleed. I go into the bedroom. George is just getting up. "When's Mom coming home?" he says.

"Dad says it's going to be a long time. Grandma Sanderson's coming today. Can you get dressed?" I'm feeling like a big brother and George will have none of it.

"I want Mother and the baby now. They can't keep her in the hospital. It isn't right. And I don't like Grandma Sanderson." George kicks at the bed and throws his shoe at the door, making a loud thunk. Dad comes into the room.

"What's going on here? Come on. Get dressed. Got to get going." Dad is partly dressed, but he looks like he needs Mom's help too. He's managed to get into his suit and tie and his hair is messed as usual. A piece of white toilet paper with a dark red spot where he cut himself is still stuck to his neck. I don't tell him to comb his hair like Mother does.

"I won't." George sits on the bed pouting. He knows how to get Dad's goat. Dad looks like he wants to say something but leaves knowing George wants him to argue.

I get dressed quickly while George sulks on the bed. I don't know how to cook oatmeal but Dad is already ahead of me. "You can eat some Wheaties and bananas. I don't have time to squeeze orange juice but maybe you can do that."

I slice the oranges in half, then stand on a chair to haul down the lime-green orange juice squeezer. I twist the oranges back and forth on the crown of the squeezer until I see orange juice and seeds fill the sides. I take a strainer from the drawer and pour the juice through so the seeds and pulp don't get mixed in the small glass. Three oranges and I've got my own drink and I'm feeling like a responsible kid.

"How's it going?" Dad says leaning back around the kitchen door frame and spotting my full glass. "Good, squeeze some for George, will you?" I say I will, thinking maybe this might take George out of his funk and into the kitchen to eat some breakfast.

"I've talked with Mrs. Pym, so she'll come down to see you boys off to school. Help her all you can. I'll see you when you get home from school. And remember, Grandma Sanderson will be here." Dad has his hat on and his briefcase in his hand, so I know he's ready to fly out the door.

"Where's my juice?" George asks after Dad has gone. I'm relieved to see him and point to his glass on the table.

I think about Grandma Sanderson coming today. She's strict and serious at the same time. I think that's because she's had a hard life. She lost her husband, Grampa Graves, when Dad was only ten years old. Mother says she did a good job of raising three kids all by herself. Two years ago she married Frankie Sanderson, and in only one year she lost him and her brother Hal in a brush fire. I guess it was pretty horrible.

Grandma Hiller is different. She jokes a lot and makes games out of almost anything, as if she can't wait for some new adventure. I figure if I can't have Mom I want my Grandma Hiller because she's Mother's mother.

Grandma Sanderson greets us at the door when we come home in the afternoon. She says a friendly "hello" and then moves into getting things organized. "Be sure to hang up your coat. Change your clothes before you go out to play. Always tell me where you'll play. Be in by five o'clock." She doesn't say anything about Mom other than "She's very sick, you know. Dad is doing all he can with school and seeing Mother. We've got to help your father."

I tell Grandma I'm going to play with Helen Johnson next door. I'm not going to play with my friends down the street. I just want to be near the house in case Dad or Mom might come home. "Be sure to be back at five o'clock," says Grandma in her firm New England voice. There's a warning in her tone I don't really understand. "Of course, I'll be back at five," I say to my-self. I'm proud that I know how to tell time. Last year, when I was six, I learned so well that Dad bought me a one dollar Elgin watch to put in the watch pocket of my Sunday trousers.

Helen and I have a good time playing, but I keep a close eye on the big clock in her kitchen. When it is five o'clock I say, "I have to be home now, good-bye," and I shoot out the door for home.

I come in the front door and yell, "I'm home, Gramma." Grandma comes out of the kitchen and her eyes look angry behind her glasses. I can't understand why. She grips my wrist tightly with strong fingers that make me yelp and walks me quickly into the kitchen to point at the clock. "The clock says three minutes past five and I know you know how to tell time. When I say five o'clock, I mean five o'clock. Now you sit in this chair and think about it." She swings me into the hard kitchen chair and I land still confused by what I've done. I do some big thinking all right. I think about Mother and the dead baby, and I so wish she was home and Grandma wasn't here.

Dad comes home after work and seeing Mother at the hospital. He looks tired. The knot on his tie is starting to slide down the front of his shirt. He places his briefcase on the floor and says, "Mother says hello to you boys and she is feeling a little better."

"Then when is she coming home?" George and I chorus together. "We miss her." I say, "Can we go see her? We want to see her."

"No, Mother's still very sick and the hospital doesn't allow children to come in. Every day I'll tell you how she is. You can count on that."

"It's not fair," George thunders. "They can't do this to us just because we're kids." He's crying loudly now and stamping his foot. I'm just standing there, the tears flowing down my cheeks. I look up at Dad. I want him to see me crying. I want him to know things are lousy at home. I want to tell him Grandma is mean, but she's standing right there.

"Time you boys get off to bed. Your Dad's had a hard day and he needs some supper." Grandma's voice is calm, not like when she bit off those angry words at me about being on time.

George and I go to our room. I'm crying now, good and loud, louder than George so Dad and Grandma can hear. I cry a little louder at first because I want to make them mad, but once I get going I can't stop. "I want Mother," I repeat over and over. The words and tears pour out of me.

Dad comes into the bedroom and starts to rub my back. "We want Mom," we shout. "I know, I know," Dad says, sounding tired and calm at the same time.

"And we don't like Grandma." I tell Dad about being late in the afternoon. "Only I wasn't late!" I shout and start crying again. Dad just sits on the edge of the bed. "I know, I know how it is," he whispers very softly, like he doesn't want Grandma to hear.

Dad must have spoken to Grandma because she seems a little softer the next day. Still, I make sure I come home early, pick up my clothes, and follow her strict routines. I watch Grandma very carefully just to see what kind of a mood she is in. She doesn't get angry like Dad. Dad just blows up. When he does that I go outside or walk away. But Grandma is different. She never blows up. I know she is angry because her chin sticks out a little more and her eyes stop moving behind her glasses.

One day after school I fall down and get a deep scrape on my knee. Two days later it doesn't look as though it is healing very well. Grandma says, "Now when you go to school, see the nurse and ask her what I should do. Don't forget."

On the way home I realize that I've forgotten to ask the nurse. I know this is much worse than being three minutes late from play. I could get a spanking or have to stay in every afternoon until Grandma Hiller comes next week. I just know it will go badly for me.

Grandma Sanderson greets me at the door, and before I can think what to say she asks, "And what did the nurse say about your cut?" She never forgets anything.

Before I know it I'm telling a fat lie, one of the best I've ever told. I turn and look straight up at her, then down at my knee, "The nurse said 'Wash it very carefully with soap and water, put on some Vaseline, and then cover it all with a Band-Aid but change the Band-Aid every day." I feel pretty proud of my lie, especially when Grandma says, "Yes, that sounds just like what we ought to do." My lie is actually a lie inside a lie because Mother would put iodine on the cut and I know Vaseline doesn't hurt. Afterwards I feel bad about telling the lie. Grandma trusts me, and every day she carefully washes the cut and changes the Band-Aid, just like the nurse said.

The next Sunday Grandma Sanderson takes the train from Grand Central Station in New York for Northampton, Massachusetts, where she lives. One day, weeks later, I realize that Dad, who is principal of the school, might have asked the school nurse, the woman I was supposed to speak to, about the advice I'd made up for Grandma's benefit. Dad and Grandma would know I'd lied for sure. I figure that was a close call.

We meet Grandma Hiller at Grand Central Station the same day Grandma Sanderson leaves. Grandma Hiller is a bouncy woman who kids us a lot. She's got lots of enthusiasm and even plays games with us. Each day Dad tells us that Mother is making good progress and that soon, any day now, she will be home.

About two weeks after Mother loses the baby Dad announces, "Today I'm going to bring Mother home. I've got a friend with a car and we'll go pick her up. She's still pretty weak and she'll need lots of help."

"We'll do anything. We'll be a big help. You'll see," I say like a grown-up.

"Yes, we'll pick up all our things, clear the table, do the dishes," George volunteers. "We'll be fast."

All afternoon we look out the front windows facing Oak Street. Finally we see a car pull up to the curb. We don't know the car and we don't know that Mother is inside until Dad jumps out the front door.

"It's Dad. It's Mom too," we shout. George races for the front door.

I stand at the window and watch Dad open the door and reach in to help Mother out of the back seat. I can't move. I don't want to move. I just want to see Mother. It's been so long since I've seen her just looking seems pretty good to me. Mother looks very thin, much thinner than when she left. She spots me in the window, smiles, and gives a weak wave with her hand.

I wrote this story a few years ago. By the time I came to the end I was surprised to find tears streaming down my face. Writing in the first person and the present tense caused me to relive the event and revealed a story to me that was much larger in the writing than in the telling.

Our family didn't deal with the death of the baby. Mother did her best when she got home from the hospital, but in one sense it was too late. My brother and I didn't get the answers we needed in those first days. Birth and death remained somehow tangled together in our minds. Mother was so careful to explain the joy and miracle of life in the womb that when death came, George and I were left with an unsolved problem. I suspect the void contained an element of fear that I could still lose my mother at some point, and it passed on into my own marriage in my fear that I might lose my wife. But I did not understand any of this until I wrote the piece.

I suspect that certain stories in our lives will always be about life and death. All our other stories about teaching and learning are enveloped by these very large stories, which form a foundation for our lives.

TRY THIS: Choose some story in your life that you suspect is more significant than you realize and try writing or telling it in the first person and present tense.

Working Next to Mother and Dad

"First, put the silverware in the bottom of the dishpan and let it soak while you wash the other dishes. Rinse, let them dry a bit, and finish off with a towel. This saves you time in the long run." Mother introduced us to the world of work through brief lectures. Each morning we had chores to do: make our beds, dump the trash, feed the dog, and dry dishes. Mother studied her routines and gave us carefully rehearsed lectures on the efficacy of certain procedures. She watched herself working, wondering all the while how to do the most menial task more efficiently.

Dad, on the other hand, dived into work with a fury. If he did the dishes, which was seldom, water flew, dishes didn't get rinsed properly, and he was done in about five minutes. We often pointed out the egg still stuck to the plate he'd just washed. Dad washed dishes the way he weeded the garden—rip, pull, heave, buzz on down the row without looking left or right. Whereas Dad was silent in his labor, Mother talked freely about life and work, and generally interviewed us about the status of our lives.

I didn't diagnose mother's modus operandi until much later. Once a day she strategically placed my brother and me next to her at the dishpan so she could carry on her informal home education. About five years ago it struck me, "Heck, those dishes would have been dry within the hour standing in the drainer. We didn't have to stand there drying each one."

One of Mother's favorite lecture topics was money—how to earn it, hold on to it, and then share it with others. Dad, on the other hand, spent whatever he had in his pocket. One day he took George and me uptown to get new baseball gloves, bats, and balls. "You didn't spend the food money did you,

Hap?" Mother moaned at Dad when we returned. She never knew when the money would run out because Dad had suddenly spent it or given it away to someone in need. She was always working at a system that would provide for the family as well as keep Dad in cash. "You mean you're out of money already?" we'd hear from the other room.

Mother kept budget envelopes—food, clothing, automobile, household, and so on—into which she allocated her cash for the week. George and I crowded around as she went through the process of helping us understand how she made decisions about money and budgets. She was determined that we wouldn't surprise our wives with big spending when we got married.

George and I were given twenty-five cents a week allowance. Inspired by Mother's lectures about budgeting our money, we pooled our allowances and set up budget envelopes of our own—church, sports, toys, presents. We could tell Mother was pleased with our efforts. Money, allowances, and work were carefully tied together with Mother's own lecture.

Mother told work stories as we dried the dishes next to her in the kitchen. "Boys, your grandfather was so efficient. I remember watching him build a simple table for Grandma so she could make pies and pastries. In no time he'd analyze how the work went, then make the table. He made a little shelf for the pans, a well for ingredients like sugar and fillings. He'd also think through the best way to make the table before he'd even made it. No wasted motion. Grandpa was always looking for better and more efficient ways to do almost anything. In his mind, with just a little design and effort, routine jobs could be done more simply."

About as soon as mother finished talking about Grandpa and efficiency, she'd discuss our father and inefficiency. This was her way of teaching when we worked with her. "Now your father is scared to death of anything mechanical as well as of the mechanics. When you go down to the garage, ask the man what's wrong with the car. Ask how his machinery works. You've got to hang around people and watch if you are ever going to learn anything."

Mother's real work model was her own mother, who was a lot like my father. When it came to pure output Grandma

Hiller and Dad were neck and neck. Mother confessed that next to Grandma she felt like a laggard. Long after my grandmother passed away my mother heard her voice checking on her work output. Perfection and accomplishment were her twin burdens. When Mother graduated third in her high school class, she raced home to tell her parents the good news. They wanted to know why she wasn't first. Mother herself was surprised to find out that she was an honor student.

"Have you done your best? Is this your best effort?" were always the underlying questions. But she never pressured me for perfection, possibly fearing I might assume the burdens passed on to her by her parents. Nevertheless, we witnessed her daily self-analysis about striving for perfection and that affected me more than any push to succeed: "The meat is overdone . . . the vegetables cooked in too much water . . . the baking powder, wrong variety . . . the apples in the pie don't have enough flavor." Everything tasted fine to me. I wondered about this unattainable thing called perfection.

The best part of my apprenticeship to Mother was witnessing her decisiveness. Every illness, meal, or outside activity required a decision. When I turned fourteen she said, "It's time you went out and got a job, Donald." Like most of her statements this was not a recommendation but an order.

"How do I do it, Mother?"

"Go downtown to the stores, ask for the manager, and say, 'I am a good worker and I wonder if you have any jobs.' Just ask." I wasn't sure I could say I was a good worker, given my work history at home, and I was surprised when Mother suggested it.

Working next to Dad, especially outdoors, was an impossible task. Keeping up with him in weeding, planting, digging, or doing yard work was hopeless. I'd weed three plants and dream while Dad did two rows. Exasperated, he would say to me, "Donald, when are you going to wake up and join us in this century?" He was always saying "Wake up!"

I'd jump as if from a stupor. "Wha' what?" Indeed, the intense pace of both my parents forced me to dream. I had to tune out the high speed activity surrounding me. I'd dream about my books, maps, hikes, fighting in the war, or building huts in the woods, anything but the task at hand. I did the same in school. My report card said "Donald could do much better if he'd stop dreaming and looking out the window."

I had to wait until I was fourteen before I tasted what it was like to work at my father's pace. Late one July afternoon in 1945 my father and I were weeding his gladiolus. Our usual procedure was to work side by side going down the rows together. We ripped away at pussley, crabgrass and pigweed. Within ten minutes Dad had a twenty-foot edge on me.

Dad didn't usually complain about my speed as long as I kept weeding. If I stopped he'd shout, "Hey, goin' to wake up?" One day, however, we both got a surprise.

A thunderstorm with black-edged thunderheads was brewing in the distance. Long gray streamers etched the sky beneath the heads, signaling rain uptown. At best, we had fifteen minutes before the deluge. "Let's finish the row before we have to quit," Dad suggested.

A fifteen-minute burst was a relief from the tedium of long hours of weeding. I could handle fifteen minutes. I roared into action, pulling and digging. For the first time in my life I didn't lose ground to my father. I pushed harder, thinking only of the task at hand. I could see I had a chance to impress him for the first time.

I remember hearing about the work ethic in Dad's family when we visited our grandmother back in Williamsburg, Massachusetts, in the summertime. Dad's father had died when he was ten years old. "People used to say my father would never walk when he could run. No one could make a buggy go faster on his milk run than my father. He'd jump from the buggy hauling the milk can, ladle out the milk and cream, and run back to the cart." Dad was introduced to farm work early and had still more responsibility after his father's death.

Dad maintained three jobs throughout his high school years. He delivered newspapers and then worked at the drugstore from seven to eight in the morning. Since the drugstore was near the school, he could also cover for half an hour at noontime and after school until five o'clock. At home he helped with chores from six to nine, when he went to work for the telephone company. Dad was the night telephone operator for Williamsburg, making seven dollars a week for covering the phones until six-thirty the next morning, when he started the day delivering newspapers. He slept on a cot in the telephone office, and when the phone clicked he'd wake up and connect the parties. Like his father, Dad never walked when he could run.

I remember my first job working for a neighbor. I mowed the grass, weeded, and did light gardening. I carried the memory of one of Dad's statements, "Now don't fall asleep on the job." I worked all morning, never stopping for fear the neighbor would think me a laggard. I rang the doorbell when I finished the work at noon. The neighbor seemed surprised and walked outside surveying what I'd done. She shook her head and mumbled to herself making little gasping noises. I was terrified. Occasionally I volunteered, "Here's a few weeds I missed over here. I'll get those as quick as I can." The woman finally turned to me and said, "I never would have believed you could have done all this in one morning and the work is excellent. Where on earth did you learn to work like that?" I was so stunned all I could answer was "I don't know."

Our parents are often our first teachers about the world of work. They establish the routines, rituals, and rationales that govern how we use each day.

When ten o'clock comes I say to myself, as my mother said to herself, "It's ten o'clock. What have you accomplished for the day?" Both of my parents followed unwritten time markers. In our family the worst thing a person could do was to waste time. They often saw my dreaming or procrastination in this light. Fortunately they didn't view reading or studying as wasting time.

Mother framed the workday according to mealtimes: breakfast at seven, lunch at noon, and supper at six. Not until recently did I realize that having set times for meals allowed us to plan our work. That is, we could all predict with assurance just what we'd be able to accomplish by six o'clock, when the evening meal was served. Both my parents were raised on small New England farms, and I suspect that their agrarian roots were a major influence in establishing the day's rhythms.

I am surprised in writing this to discover how closely work, time, meals, and money were tied together. Behind each of those words I sense the word *rhythm*. Each day had its pace for working and learning. I often wonder about the constantly interrupted days of our children's lives. Our chores were important benchmarks in learning how to use time in school and in preparing us for the world of work.

TRY THIS: Recall a time when you worked next to your parents, another family member, or a neighbor, where you could feel yourself learning about work. Tell the story of one of those occasions. Consider how your early learning about the world of work is still with you today.

Uncle Nelson

The brown felt hat was his trademark. You'd start at that hat a quarter of a mile out to sea and check his casual lean into the wind as his long arm commanded the scull oar in the stern. His name was Horatio Nelson Wilbur. We called him Uncle Nelson.

At seventy-six years of age he could kick the top of a doorjamb, scratch his left ear with his right toe, scull a boat, tell jokes, sing lurid sea shanties, comment on the world scene, or sum up a personality in three words. I first got to know my uncle when he hired my brother and me to clean his rowboats and collect money for his summer boat business. I was twelve years old and needed to learn what schools couldn't teach.

At the end of the day we settled up the money while he inspected the boats. Our share was 10 percent of the proceeds. A day's work from five A.M. until seven P.M. brought us about two dollars each, on lean days as little as seventy-five cents.

"Not much today, Uncle Nelson," I'd say.

"Better than getting kicked in the ass with a cold boot on a frosty morning," he'd reply.

That was typical of Uncle Nelson, black sheep among the relatives on my mother's side, a slight bit of irreverence to sum things up. He stood a lean six feet, two inches, and with a cigar tucked in the side of his mouth, he could smoke, spit, and tell stories at the same time. My family was uneasy about our association. Uncle Nelson drank, cussed, gambled, plastered his walls with pictures of nude women, and worst of all, voted for a democrat, Franklin Delano Roosevelt.

Uncle Nelson had to leave school when he was twelve to work on his father's farm, yet he was one of the most informed and remarkable teachers I have ever known. For twenty years at election time, the *New Bedford Standard Times* sent a reporter to get a "state of the nation" interview at Uncle Nelson's shack on the shore. People wanted to know what the old man had to say.

Although Uncle Nelson could be instructive with words, he believed that people were best taught through demonstration. This was true whether he wanted to help someone or teach a kind of moral lesson. During the Depression Uncle Nelson helped everyone he could. Men came without money asking to take his boats out to catch enough fish to feed their families. They didn't have to plead. He just said, "Take the boat, catch all you can. When you have enough money, stop by." He knew it would be a long time before they had any.

A well-to-do couple, Norman and Bernice, had also fallen on hard times during the Depression. They lost everything, with the exception of some fine furniture, during the stock market crash of '29. But Nelson had a cottage they could live in rent free. In this way they could maintain some dignity during the summer while Norman looked for work.

Norman and Bernice maintained more than appearances. They held parties, showed off their old way of living, and worst of all, didn't clean their outhouse. Uncle Nelson patiently reminded them that "they oughter get to it before the end of July." I remember one hot day the first week in August when Uncle Nelson muttered about Norman and Bernice's air force as he brushed flies from his dinner table.

Several days later my brother and I walked around the corner of the barn and witnessed one of Uncle Nelson's teaching exhibitions. Norman and Bernice, nattily attired in whites and lemons, were in the midst of a lawn party, pouring drinks into tall glasses under flower-covered umbrellas. With the wind blowing from the southwest a brisk fifteen to twenty knots, Uncle Nelson set himself to the windward of the party and dutifully cleaned the errant outhouse. Then, when his wheelbarrow was full, he calmly pushed his way through the shocked partygoers. As he drew abreast of my brother and me, but still within earshot of the party, he triumphantly proclaimed the indignity of his evidence. He pointed to the lumps in the wheelbarrow and cackled loud enough for everyone to hear, "There's Norman and there's Bernice, oops . . . there's Norman again."

Pomposity, injustice, and inflated egos were his instructional specialties. At the end of my freshman year in college, sporting new vocabulary words, cut-off shorts, and a loud T-shirt, I made my way up the beach on my first day back at the shore. I couldn't find Uncle Nelson so I headed up past the boathouse figuring he might be out clamming, since it was low tide.

I found him under his brown felt hat, hefting a sledgehammer as he worked on a new sea wall for Mrs. Fitzsimmons.

"Hi Don," he hailed me. "Hell of a day, ain't it?"

"Sure is," I said.

"A hell of a day to die," he countered. "I'm eighty-three years old this next Lincoln's birthday and this sonofabitchin' boulder ain't right for a man my age. You're a young bull. You split and I'll rest a sec."

I stripped off my T-shirt, flexed my muscles, fresh from strong college workouts, and eyed the three-foot-high boulder with a measure of confidence. If Uncle Nelson thought I could do it, I'd do it with dispatch.

I positioned my feet and swung at the center of the boulder with all the ego-driven force I could muster. The sledge struck the rock but the rock struck back, sending a return force through the head of the sledge that vibrated up the shaft until it reached my ears with a high-pitched, ringing "wheee." The sledge jumped from my hands, landing in a pile of small rocks some six feet from where I stood. My shoulders felt as though they'd been driven up into my chin. I heard a hoarse "heh heh" off to my right.

Embarrassed, I swung at the rock again but with less confidence and force. Again the sledge dropped to the ground. He chuckled and said, "Poor bastard thinks he's strong. You may have muscles, my boy, but for a college fella you've got an unused brain." He stood up and waggled a long finger at the end of a gangly arm.

"Now watch. First you look the boulder over. Now, you see this seam here crossed by this gravely stuff? That's a weak point. Take this sledge and tap it just so." Holding the sledge like a putter at the U.S. Open, Uncle Nelson tapped the spot under instruction and the boulder cracked and dropped into two pieces.

"Sonofabitch, damned if it ain't goin' to be a good day after all," trumpeted Uncle Nelson.

I wasn't so sure.

One of the reasons we learn so much in our family or on the job is that we hang around people who show us how they think. Uncle Nelson taught constantly through demonstration. He was a pungent character who provided a spicy flavor to living that was tailor-made for young adolescents trying to grow up. In the midst of seeming irreverence and spoofing was a rock-ribbed honesty that has stayed with my brother and me over a lifetime. This is not to say that our parents weren't honest or didn't teach us what honesty meant. But away from home Uncle Nelson showed us the meaning of integrity when he didn't charge men who needed fish for food. What he taught was definite and solid and could be summoned at a moment's notice.

TRY THIS: Recall an important teacher—a neighbor, a friend, or a member of your extended family—who taught you how to live in the world and whose demonstrations you still carry with you.

How to Catch a Shark

The summer of 1949 was an unusually hot one in New England. One heat wave after another drove people to the shore. I was lucky to be living in the last house at the end of Wilbur's Point in Fairhaven, Massachusetts. When not working at my regular job uptown, before entering my sophomore year of college in the fall, I spent as much time as I could fishing the waters of Buzzards Bay. The heat warmed the water of the bay and with the warm water came fish species not common to our area. Even more unusual were large numbers of blue sharks.

One day a fisherman hauled his boat up on our runway. I could see him waving his arms, extending them as wide as he could while he spoke with my Uncle Nelson. I moved closer and picked up on their conversation. "First I saw a fin and then I saw the whole a him. God, he went from here to there," he said, pointing from himself to a post eight feet distant. That was about the middle of July.

In August the sightings became commonplace. We worried that the sharks might be eating the gamefish we enjoyed catching, like bluefish or striped bass.

About the third week of August we were trolling for stripers off West Island, which stood about two miles east of where we lived at Wilbur's Point. We liked to troll in close to the rocks because stripers usually hang out near rocks, which provide their kind of feed. Since it was low tide I stood in the bow looking down and pointing out the rocks so we wouldn't shear a pin on the outboard motor. Suddenly, two large white shapes surged off and away from our approach. Although I didn't see their dorsal fins I knew they were sharks. The stripers wouldn't enjoy the shark's company. We returned home knowing there'd be no more fishing that day.

My friend Bob McCarthy and I stood around the boathouse talking about the sharks. Jake Brightman, a well-known and successful fisherman at the Point, joined in. "You can catch them, you know. Takes a good rig and a long wait, but it can be done. Take a look at this." Jake ducked inside the little shanty we called a boathouse and returned with a large hook and chain. It was the largest hook I'd ever seen. The hook was heavy steel, an eighth of an inch in diameter with a good three inches from the barb to the shank of the hook. Attached to the hook was a quarter-inch chain about twelve feet long. "You got this chain so's the shark can't cut the line. What happens is soon's they get hooked they whirl around to bite what's holding them. They can't bite through the chain. Now, you go out there with some good bait on this hook and a long quarter-inch line attached to the chain and you just might get something."

I wasn't the best fisherman at the Point by any means. I'd go out with my brother, George, Dad, or anyone else to troll for stripers or bluefish. They'd catch fish and I'd come home without any. People like me were called Jonahs after the Bible story. The biblical story had it that Jonah was thrown overboard because he was bringing bad luck to the people in his boat. Not only would I probably not catch any fish, but I might affect the luck of the other fisherman in the boat. As I stared at that rig, I began to imagine how I might be regarded if I ever came in with one of those big blue sharks. I was going out with a young woman who might also cast a different eye on me if I returned with one of those big soakers. I felt the testosterone kick in.

"What do you think, Bob? Want to try it?" Bob was about three years my junior but I could see he was interested.

"I've got a .22 rifle," Bob remarked enthusiastically, "so if we do catch one we could shoot it." I liked that idea because I hadn't yet figured out how to kill a shark if we ever got one on the line. Up to that point my South Sea story knowledge had me striking the shark with a large knife, and I didn't see how that could be accomplished.

"Right, good idea. So, we've got to put together a rig this afternoon. Then we can head out tomorrow morning." I queried Jake still further about how to prepare.

"I recommend a fresh bluefish head for the bait. Fresh and bloody, that ought to attract them. You need your line and plenty of it, at least three hundred feet of quarter inch, all laid out carefully, because if you get one on, you don't want to get caught in a singing line.

We waited for an incoming tide and using Bob McCarthy's motor, we headed over to West Island in one of Uncle Nelson's hardy twelve-foot skiffs. I figured we might as well drop a line where I'd seen the two sharks the day before. We set up for a long wait. Bob brought his portable radio and I had a good book. I took an ice pick and poked holes in the bluefish head to make sure it was oozing blood. I hooked the head, hiding the barb so it wouldn't show. Then I twirled the head with chain and line and gave it a good heave off the bow about thirty feet away.

We discussed our strategy if we got a hit. My job was to put on the gloves to protect my hands from rope burns on a fast-moving line. I'd set the hook, let out plenty of line, then cleat it on the forward thwart of the skiff. Bob's job was to get the motor out of the water and pull the anchor. We didn't want the shark to get tangled in either the anchor line or the propeller. Instead of using the forward thwart to cleat the anchor, we tied the anchor line loosely around the middle seat so it was well within Bob's reach and could be quickly hauled in.

I propped two boat cushions against the forward thwart and reached for my book. Bob occupied the rear seat with his radio. I'd just finished putting the cushions in place when a large dorsal shark fin poked out of the water, cruised by our boat, and disappeared. My heart started to thump so fast I could scarcely breathe. "Did you see that!" Bob yelled.

"Did I ever!" We both forgot about books and radios and sat eyeing the quarter-inch line to see if it moved. Nothing happened. After a half-hour of tense readiness we returned to our original plan for a long wait. I sat reading C. S. Forester's *The Midshipman.*

Several hours went by as we waited in the afternoon sun. Suddenly Bob called me from my reading. "I think the line is moving." It was slowly passing over my shoulder, the thwart, and into the water.

I got up, turned and put on my gloves, and watched the

line move slowly out of the tub. This was not drift caused by the boat; the line was moving away from us in a clear direction. Gently, I pulled back on the line, feeling resistance from whatever was on the other end. "Well, here goes."

I set my feet and yanked on the line as hard as I could to set the hook. Instantly, a shark broke from the water, tail-walking above the surface, its entire body almost coming clear. I could hear the chain rattle as it shook its head to free itself from the barb and line. But the hook held firm as the shark sped for open water. By this time Bob had the anchor up and the motor free.

It is hard to know how fast the shark was towing us as we sped along, parallel to the shore of West Island. Clam diggers gave us surprised looks as we cleared the end of the island heading for open water. The motor was pulled up and we had no oars. It was as if the boat was being moved by some unseen force.

About a quarter of a mile out to sea, the line suddenly went slack. "We've lost it, Bob," I said sorrowfully. "Guess it got loose from the hook." Once again it seemed that my Jonah-like luck had returned. I was nonchalantly pulling in the line when suddenly it jumped from my hands, nearly knocking me off balance. "It's still on!" I shouted. Later, I learned that sharks will rest on the bottom when they get tired from pulling.

The shark headed farther out to sea, but after another quarter mile it changed strategy. It began to circle the boat in an attempt to work the hook free.

"We're going to need to get it closer in for a shot," Bob volunteered. At this point the shark was about a hundred feet away. I pulled in on the line gradually until the shark was about twenty-five feet away.

"Oh, it's a good one," I figured at least nine feet long. Bob loaded his rifle and fired. He hit the shark and the shark jumped but not nearly as much as when I first set the hook. We worked him in closer for more shots. Now blood from the shark filled the water in a red cloud. I began to worry about other sharks, which were legendary for feasting on their own kind, but none appeared.

We finally got the exhausted but still living shark alongside the boat. To make sure it wouldn't get away, I fashioned a lasso, passed it slowly over the tail, and pulled taut. We had the shark fore and aft. Bob killed it with his rifle. Now we had a ten-foot shark to haul into a twelve-foot boat.

We motored back to the West Island shore where the clammers came running to get a look at what pulled us to sea. We both swaggered a little as we stepped out of the skiff onto the beach. "Yup, we got 'em on this line, hooked 'em good." I spoke nonchalantly while pointing at the bloody blue shark alongside the skiff.

"You mean there are sharks like this in the water where we were clamming?" one woman gasped, her eyes darting around to note the location of her children.

"They're all over the place. These sharks especially like the sand shoals where you were clamming. At low tide they cruise in to soak up the sun in the warm water."

"Good grief, why aren't there signs here to tell us about this?" a man in a straw hat added, in an angry voice. "These could be man eaters! Look at the size of it! Look at the teeth!"

I was so happy we had caught the shark, I wasn't concerned about the safety of the crowd. "Bob, know what? Let's like put the shark in the boat with the head right up there on the forward thwart so that when we come in that shark is staring everyone in the face. Let 'em see the teeth."

"Yeah." But the dead weight of the shark complicated our efforts to get the carcass in the skiff. I kept eyeing the head to make sure those menacing teeth wouldn't come to life, although clearly we never would have lost it, since the hook attached to the chain had disappeared down its gullet. When we finally managed to get the head propped up on the thwart, we were surprised that the rest of our trophy stretched clear to the back seat. I walked around to the bow to check the effect of the shark when we reached the Point and the boathouse. I felt as though I'd finally shed my Jonah curse.

A crowd gathered as we hauled the skiff with the shark propped in the prow up the runway. I looked down and was surprised to find that the quarter-inch line was severed. Evidently, the shark's jaws had relaxed in death or the line had rubbed against the teeth and their sharpness had severed it.

My family arrived but I didn't see my girlfriend. In time the word would spread. I had figured I'd pull out the shark's teeth with pliers and see about making a shark's tooth necklace like those I'd seen in stores uptown. My triumph would forever bedeck my girlfriend's neck as she told the story to her friends.

We hauled the shark up over the boathouse door. Cameras popped away at Bob and me standing on either side of the shark. Those moments were the high point of our victory.

The next day I tried to extract the teeth with pliers, but I had pulled only three when my gloves and hands were so cut by the razor-sharp teeth that I abandoned the project. We cut thick shark steaks and tried to cook them in a skillet. We'd provide for our families. Within minutes we were driven from the house by clouds of urine-smelling steam. It seems that sharks have no waste-filtering system. As we heaved the steaks into the bushes I think I heard the shark laugh.

I needed this story more at eighteen than I do now. Then I needed to feel as though I had done something significant. A large shark with razor-sharp teeth propped in the prow of the small skiff provided an ego-boosting image.

When I went to Bates College in the fall I retold the story numerous times to enhance a daredevil image that didn't really exist apart from the story. I'd take out the photo of Bob and me with the shark in between us.

I told the story again when I began dating my future wife. I still needed to be macho man, this time in the eyes of a woman. Of course, she soon grew tired of the story and was embarrassed when I'd tell it in company. "Wanna hear the story about the time I caught a man-eating shark?" She'd head for the kitchen.

By the time I crossed the threshold of forty I seldom told the story anymore. The child inside was growing up and no longer needed a shark to give him stature. I think of big game hunters posing beside their tigers, lions, and bears.

I suspect that children, like each of us, have stories that help them to feel a bit taller among their peers. These stories may have a short life, but at the time they help us to grow.

Try this: Think of a story you've told over the years. Has your need for the story changed? Tell the story and comment on its place in your life.

Shaving

I figure that from the time I started at fifteen until this morning I've shaved about 15,370 times. Shaving ought to be routine stuff by now, but it isn't. The act itself is routine but getting there to look at myself in the mirror isn't.

I couldn't wait to shave. When I was fifteen, I spent hours in front of the mirror eagerly eyeing the tiny black hairs on my upper lip and regularly checked in with Dad about cutting them off. My friends swapped stories in cracking adolescent voices about shaving and dates with girls, and checked each other in the locker room for further evidence of hair in any location that hinted of manhood. I wanted to join them but had little hair to show, and my voice was stuck in the tenor range. No change.

When the moment finally came I borrowed Dad's Gillette razor and rub-on shaving cream. Dad showed me how to unscrew the outer plate, enter the single-edge blade, and soak the two square inches of hair on my upper lip with hot water. Shaving the upper lip, forever the riskiest place, is a tough way to start. I am stuck with finger dexterity that places me at the lowest percentile level of all humans. How to keep from nicking my nose or lip with a few short strokes is a sensitive issue even today. The razor is still a deadly weapon, especially the Gillette razor of forty-seven years ago.

I rolled my lips in and curled them around my teeth for maximum protection, which served to move my nose higher and out of the way as I rubbed on the shaving cream. My first shave required four strokes. I checked the mirror: no hairs, no manhood. But at least I had a story to tell my friends: I'd joined the club. I'd also joined Gillette as sponsor of Don Dunphy during his broadcast of Friday night fights on the radio.

Shaving takes longer now than in 1945. I started using a brush and shaving soap in the spring of my freshman year in college. My beard stiffened and the rub-on cream in the Gillette tube didn't work nearly as well. And I liked the feel of the warm water and the brush.

Getting to the sink to shave started to get difficult about the time I had to shave every day. Routine acts requiring daily obeisance always recall my mother's voice ("Be sure to take your bath, scrub behind your ears, and brush your teeth before you get into bed"). Once I stand before the mirror and begin to use the hot water and the brush, the routine becomes pure pleasure. I enjoy rituals once I am involved in them. They allow me to think about other things.

I shave about the same way each day. Shaving is an automatic act that allows me to forget the outward journey of the moving razor and concentrate on the inward journey of thought. Once the lather is on, I set the right sideburn with one downward stroke and work down my right cheek to the jawline. I used to be pretty careful about the sideburns. I'd do the right and angle an eye before setting the left. That framed the territory. But in the last few years, and especially in retirement, I'm less fussy, not only about the sideburns but about the entire shave. I've got a "that's-the-way-I-am" outlook and it feels good.

I reach underneath my jaw to my neck and stroke upward, first on the right side, then on the left. I stretch my head back to pull the skin taut for easy shaving. Whiskers on the jaw line, both left and right, seem to be the most stubborn, and take working and reworking. I often have to lather the jawline a second time before I can finish the shave. I still leave my upper lip, the very place I began to shave forty-seven years ago, for last.

An audience helps. Children, and now grandchildren, stand on a chair or the toilet seat to watch the operation. Their fascination is particularly acute between the ages of three and six. The razor swings through the white cream in swaths along my face. "Does it hurt, Grandpa?" they'll ask. Occasionally, I'll nick a piece of skin or a mosquito bite; they watch pop-eyed as the creamy lather becomes bright red. "Oooh, Grandpa's bleedin'," they shout, and I hear the pounding of feet as more grandchildren arrive to peek. The opportunity to see a little blood is enough to keep them coming back again and again.

This piece represents a different kind of learning. I've taken shaving, something very routine, something I do from day to day, and followed its evolution. Since my involvement has extended over a fifty-two-year period, it has naturally accumulated a collection of stories.

Knowing how we do things, even the most minor ones, shows us how we learn. I enjoy taking very routine things—brushing my teeth, washing dishes, cleaning the car, or shopping for food—and analyzing them to achieve more efficient operation. I watch myself while this is going on. There is a good chance that you too have learned how to conduct simple operations like these more effectively over the years.

TRY THIS: Choose something you've done every day for a long time (making a bed, eating breakfast, or driving a car). First write about what you actually do, notice how this has changed over the years, and look for stories that tell about those changes. Although you can do this orally, this particular exercise works much better if it is written.

Singing into Learning

I liked the Spanish language but I didn't like Señor Muller, the new third-year Spanish teacher. Fresh out of Montclair State Teachers College, he wanted to work miracles with seniors at Tenafly High School in New Jersey. When he taught, he leaned into his work, speaking fluent Spanish in a first sergeant's voice. Words flowed from his prominent mouth, positioned beneath large brown eyes in a small head. A thin man, his bony elbows and long fingers seemed to push us into the language.

I missed Señor LaCoste, my second-year teacher, who had left Tenafly after a dispute with the new principal. Señor La-Coste was an easy-going Basque from Argentina who doubled as the high school tennis coach. His cousin was the famous French tennis player, Roberto LaCoste, known as the Bounding Basque. Señor LaCoste spoke Spanish with a slow nasal twang that was invitational in its genial pace.

Señor Muller assigned us a novel to read in a week's time. I barely made headway with two pages a night; the rest of the class stumbled along as I did. Somewhere in the middle of October he announced that we would abandon the novel, muttering to himself, "I thought this was Spanish III." Instead, we would sing in Spanish. "You'll like these songs. Listen." He sang at the top of his lungs, "Besame, besame mucho, como si fuera esta noche la ultima vez." (Kiss me, kiss me more, as if tonight was the last time.) His long, thin fingers moved up and down the keyboard. This was unapologetic singing and playing.

I looked over at Jack Merritt in the next seat. We snickered together. We were embarrassed to see another male unashamedly undressing himself with his voice before the entire class. We couldn't look at Señor Muller. There was something about another man singing that made us very uncomfortable. I almost wished we were back struggling with the novel.

"And listen to this one. This is a cowboy song from Mexico. 'Ay Jalisco, Jalisco, tu tienes tu novia, tu novia que es Guadalajara.'" (Ay Jalisco, Jalisco, you have your sweetheart, your sweetheart who is Guadalajara.) He spun around on the piano bench. "You try it. Now, with me." I looked at Jack again: no snickers, just terror. Señor had either been in this situation before or he was just too inexperienced to realize how embarrassed and terrified we all were. He wanted us to undress with him. He put the words on the board and conducted and sang at the piano. "Everyone, now . . ." A few female voices joined in with Señor Muller, by the second line perhaps another four, and by the time we hit the refrain, "Ay Jalisco, no te rajes, me sale del alma, gritar con calor, abrir todo pecho, pa echar este grito, que lindo is Jalisco," we had all begun to come out from under our egos and try a line or two. By the time we hit the refrain the third time, we had become a class. The upward spiral of a group of seniors in third-year Spanish began at that point. An old Mexican cowboy song had brought us together.

Señor Muller was obviously in his element as a Spanish song-and-dance man. He continued to speak in Spanish about the new songs, the drama and enjoyment that could be ours in this class. He explained the background to the songs. At Christmastime he introduced Spanish carols, particularly those of Cuba, since his wife, the daughter of the famous philosopher, Ortega y Gasset, was from Cuba. He spoke of the familiar ties between the people, the Virgin, and the Christ Child.

"Listen to this." He sang, "La Virgen lava panales." We joined in, following the verses on the board. "Do you know what *panales* are?" We didn't, of course. "*Panales* are diapers. The Virgin is washing diapers, is what the song is all about." We laughed and sang on.

"Here's another." In mock serious tones he sang as if in priestly incantation, "San Jose al Nino Jesus. Le Dio un beso en la cara. Y en ese momento El Nino dijo, 'Que me pinchas con la barba!'" (St. Joseph looks down on the baby Jesus and gives him a kiss on the face. Then the baby Jesus says, "Hey, you're pinching me with your beard!") With the final line, Señor Muller, a consummate actor, shifted to a child's bellow: "Que me pinchas con la barba!"

Music became such a central part of Spanish III, we'd often ask, "Are we going to sing today?"

"No, we've got to work."

"Why not?" we argued. "Look how much Spanish we are learning."

"All right, here's a bargain. If you work extra hard Monday through Thursday, we'll sing every Friday." We agreed and most of the time we had music on Fridays. We pushed hard for excellence in reading, grammar, and writing. Students who didn't finish their work were admonished by others for fear we'd miss our Friday singing.

Somewhere after Christmas Señor Muller's name was shortened to "El Sen." I think he liked it—as long as we kept on working.

Señor Muller's singing is still part of me and I remember the words and music in that class fifty years ago as if it were yesterday. (I've written the text from memory; for those of you who know the songs, please forgive the inaccuracies.)

I remember using Beatles songs in the 1960s to teach English in our ESL classes and how quickly the joy and rhythm of the music caught hold. We often forget the power of song and poetry to draw us into a new language and culture. In Señor Muller's classroom, we became an instant community. He knew that eventually we'd be captured by the music and pressed on, ignoring our first reactions.

Good teachers have always multiplied the sensory aspects of learning. Learning a language can be an abstract proposition. The words in a Spanish book sit on the page waiting for understanding. Children just learning to read examine the abstract squiggles waiting for pictures that never appear. Señor Muller broke through our adolescent embarrassment with his own joyful love of the language. Suddenly language and culture were not

Learning the
Old-Fashioned Way

"All right, let's put your brains on paper. There will be six questions. You won't need more than one line to answer each one. Write as if you were writing a telegram, ten cents a word. I'll deduct one point for each unnecessary word."

Professor Berkleman announced the dreaded pop quiz in his typical dramatic fashion. He strode into class, put his books on the desk, spun around, and with brown eyes shining, delivered the news: "Pop quiz." He enjoyed the taste of tension so much that a spray of saliva was released with the plosive "p." Thin, balding, with a mustache and wire rim glasses, he bore in my eyes a slight resemblance to Heinrich Himmler, the famed head of the German Gestapo.

"Berkie," as he was called on good days, taught the old-fashioned way, through precision, memorization, and intimidation. Class preparation for his course on Western World Literature had to be razor sharp. Rapid, random questions forced us to sit on the edge of our chairs. "Don, give three examples of Homeric epithets from Ulysses." If I paused he'd dismiss me with a glaring flick of his eye and go on to the next student. I was a sophomore transfer to Bates College in Lewiston, Maine. My peers warned me about Professor Berkleman: "You'll learn as you never have before, but he'll scare you half to death. Any course with him is worth two with anyone else. Be sure to take a light load when you enroll in Western World Lit."

Stories about him were legendary. Professor Berkleman didn't have a doctorate, and we all wondered why. One student, who had already completed his course and had nothing to lose, asked him, "Professor, can you tell me why you don't have a doctor's degree?"

"Who would examine me?"

When he wasn't asking questions he paced the room extolling the wonders of literature and language. "Listen to Homer's Greek, listen for the sounds of the sea on the beach, the sounds of the flowing sea." He accented the alliterative Greek memorized years ago. He wrote the lines on the board. I memorized the sounds and I still have them today. "Learn the language. Then you can carry it with you for the rest of your life."

"You buy your book for ten dollars at the bookstore, but by the end of this semester it ought to be worth fifty because of the notes you've jotted in the margins. Don't ever read without your pen. The pen is an extension of your mind. Busy pen. Busy mind." He produced as many homilies about learning as he did about literature.

"Your assignment tonight is to write a scene that Shakespeare might have written. Take an unwritten, off-stage action and put it into iambic pentameter. You get a plus if it could have been Shakespeare, a check if it might have been Shakespeare on a bad day, and a minus if I determine you are an impostor of the worst sort."

I worked until the wee hours of the morning trying to be worthy of Shakespeare when I was actually more worried about being worthy of Berkie's steely-eyed judgment. I wrote an off-stage scene about King Henry V crossing the English channel to France, ending with what I thought was an elegant rhyming couplet. I was overjoyed to receive a check but opposite the couplet he'd written one word: Facile. He read scenes aloud from the two students who'd received a plus. "This is worthy of Shakespeare and I defy any scholar to tell the difference."

The pop quiz was his hallmark. Six pop quizzes, contributing one third of the total grade, were distributed across each semester. The class game was to tell when the quiz would be given. If three weeks went by without a quiz, the pressure became unbearable. Raucous laughter or chest-tightening silence greeted his entrance into the classroom.

The quizzes had to be taken. If for some reason a student was absent the day of a quiz, that used up one of the allowed graces. Twice in a semester a student could go to Professor

46

Berkleman before class and say, "I'm not prepared to take a quiz today," but only twice for whatever reason.

One poor student found out how clearly the professor stayed with his fixed format. He had already used up his two graces and approached the professor before class with an authentic tale of woe. "Excuse me, Professor Berkleman, but I was unable to study all last evening because I was throwing up." His eyes were dark and drawn, accenting his pale complexion. "I didn't want to miss class but I can't take the quiz if there is one."

Professor fired back, "Nonsense, John Keats wrote some of his best poetry when he was spitting blood." That ended the discussion. However, there was no quiz that day.

I could never teach in the manner of Professor Berkleman. At the same time, I know that I owe much of my appreciation of English literature to him. I felt a certain terror as I worried about pop quizzes and pushed at details in order to be prepared in class. I memorized long passages of literary texts and still carry them, tongue ready.

I am fascinated by the campus lore about him. A good friend from my hometown took his class ten years before I arrived on campus. "Wait 'til you have Berkleman," he said, and told a story about a pop quiz.

I've long held a theory that the unwritten lore that precedes teachers into the classroom in the stories people tell about them to a large degree determines how much long-term learning will follow. Indeed, a class of second-graders in a new school will have started to compile opinions and facts about you as a teacher by recess on the first day: "What's she like? Did you notice what she's wearing? I don't like the sound of her voice. She really jumped on Ricky. I think she's going to be strict." Later, these fragments will become stories, stories that last.

TRY THIS: Think back to teachers whose personalities were very different from your own and yet you learned. Tell a story about one of those teachers. Why do you think you learned?

Try to remember a legendary teacher whose lore preceded him or her into the classroom. Tell that story.

Lessons in Failure

The dean put me on academic probation the last semester of my senior year in college. I was an English major and during the first semester wrote a thesis on tragedy. I wrote about Prince Andrey Bolkonsky in *War and Peace*—and became a near statistic of the literary form I tried to cover. In my essay I struggled to come to terms with death, my right to kill, and conscientious objection. I had seven months left to clear my thinking before the government sent me out to kill others in Korea. My professor, Dr. Wrenn (a pseudonym), gave me a D+ and wrote only one comment: "Please change your typewriter ribbon." That one painful incident affected me as a learner and a teacher for the next forty years.

I suspect I was more naive and romantic than most students when I entered college in 1948. I had decided that college was the place to struggle with moral issues and big questions: What did it mean to be a true citizen of the world? (I joined the World Federalists.) What position should I adopt regarding nuclear weapons and national armaments? What does it mean to be a Christian? Is it right to kill? What does it mean to be human and express oneself? Each morning at six I'd head to the basement of the dormitory where it was quiet to study all sorts of books and materials not included in the college curricula. I'd heal myself and the world, all at the same time. I selected English as the best major for the trip. Thus, every article, book, or course I applied to my "big questions" and what I should do with my life. The institution wanted to know if I knew the facts, the real stuff that constituted learning. I started with emotion, angst, passion, and struggle; facts could come later. A self-centered learner, I assumed that my professors shared my quest to use writing to deal with real issues and would be interested in my search.

In September 1951, at the start of our senior year, Ted Davey and I stood in front of the mailboxes in Chase Hall at Bates College in Lewiston, Maine. We were both on the track team and Ted had taught me how to throw the javelin. We wondered if we'd receive mail the first day of classes and watched the glass window of our boxes for letters. A white diagonal line soon appeared in Ted's.

We teased Ted about receiving a letter from a girlfriend. "Who is she, Ted? Some kind of summer you must have had." Ted didn't enjoy dating girls. He wore horn-rimmed glasses over slightly crossed eyes. He'd shout downeast style from his window to dorm mates leaning out second story windows, "Get your head inside; don't you know there's woodpeckers out there?"

Ted broke the seal on the envelope. "They can't do this to me. I've been ordered to report for active duty. My reserve unit has been called up." Five minutes later he returned from telephoning his unit. "They can. I've got to go home." That was the last time I saw Ted Davey. He was killed eight weeks later by a sniper in Korea while directing traffic as a military policeman.

The following June I was slated to join Ted in the military. Most college students in 1952, unless they were in reserve units, were deferred from enlistment until graduation. I struggled with conscientious objection. Ted's death, and my reading of Tolstoy's position on violence, churned within me. Dr. Wrenn, my advisor and the chair of the department, outwardly a mild-mannered, bespectacled professor, admonished me against studying the Russian authors. "You ought to study authors in your own language and culture before taking on the Russians." I went ahead with Dostoevsky and Tolstoy anyway.

I couldn't leave the Russians alone. I believed that Russian writers struggled more viscerally with life, death, killing, forgiveness, and restitution than Dickens or Wordsworth. Russian authors asked questions more closely allied with my own struggles, especially Tolstoy. Professors were less attuned to conscientious objection during the Korean War than during Vietnam, when so many students opposed the war. My professor was more worried about my poor writing and lack of interest in British writers, his own personal area of expertise. The only marks he made on my thesis were for thirty-six errors in grammar, spelling, and punctuation. (There were actually many more he didn't circle.) He made no response to my struggle with conscientious objection and death, or Ted's death.

I exploded. I railed to my roommates. I spouted righteous epithets and flunked three out of four end-of-semester exams a week later. I may have thought that failure was my way to get back at the college. The registrar looked at my grades and did her duty. A brief letter went to my parents stating that their son Donald had six months to erase his academic probation or he wouldn't graduate.

I calmed down enough to graduate and enlisted for a four-year hitch in the U.S. Coast Guard. I figured I wouldn't have to kill anyone if I was stationed in New England, the most likely Coast Guard assignment in those days. The combination of my feelings of humiliation from Bates and my desire to continue to learn on my own pushed me into several major study binges over the next four years; that meant an average of thirty study hours a week.

I shifted my energies from resolving the conscientious objection dilemma to searching for moral authority and a better focus on the details of knowledge and learning. I've always learned better when I focus; taking five subjects at one time in high school or college simply wasn't my way to learn. I figured that the facts of learning would provide some measure of confidence, which might lead in a vocational direction when I left the service. I didn't know the meaning of a writing voice, although I did have an editorial on outlawing the Communist Party accepted by the *Christian Science Monitor*. I developed a reputation for writing letters that helped six out of seven sailors get hardship discharges.

I was also in love with Betty Lewis, a presidential scholar at Bates and now my wife of forty-four years. I feared her knowledge of my grades and worked to show her I could learn. The first year I studied psychology: Freud, Brill, Jung, and others. The next year and a half I studied anatomy and physiology with the base doctor and slipped out on liberty to participate in post-mortems at Faulkner hospital. I seriously considered medical school but knew I had little chance of entry with my English background and poor college grades.

I switched to studying Russian, took a night course at Harvard, and studied both the language and the culture for the next year. A tutor helped me to learn the language. I traveled to New York to see about studying at the Russian cultural center at Columbia as well as at Harvard. Again, memories of Bates and my inability to write made me draw back. I simply couldn't handle a rejection letter.

Six months before I was mustered out of the U.S. Coast Guard I latched on to studying reading in the public schools. I visited elementary schools where my father was superintendent and observed teachers teaching children to read. The need for teachers in 1956 was so great, they'd take nearly anyone who had a college degree. I was accepted into an eight-week teacher preparation course in Hyannis, Massachusetts, sponsored by Bridgewater State College. I found out that I could teach.

Although I was able to create enthusiasm for learning in my classroom, I give myself a failing grade for teaching writing. I taught as I was taught, maliciously correcting the papers of my sixth- and seventh-grade students. I was uneasy about my practice but I simply had no other teaching model to follow. Twenty years later, when I conducted a study for the Ford Foundation, I learned that parents want their children to be taught as they were taught, even though their own learning experiences were filled with horror stories. Adults abused in their own childhood tend to replicate their own experiences; they've witnessed no other alternative.

During my first years of teaching I continued work on my master's degree in education at Bridgewater State. I took a required course in research from Dr. Jordan Fiore, a history professor, and wrote a major paper, "Leo Tolstoy—Neglected Educator." I knew of Tolstoy's progressive school at Yasnaya Polyana in the early 1860s. Many of his practices would still be called progressive in the 1950s, when I took the course.

I spent hours in Widener Library at Harvard doing research in Tolstoy's journals and his writing for children. The paper came back with a rather lengthy comment praising my work and the underlined words "You must publish this paper!" Although I was pleased with the professor's comments, I did nothing to push publication. I thought the remarks gratuitous. I still believed Dr. Wrenn, my college professor at Bates, who remained my mental companion six years later. Even though he wrote only one line, a line not related to the content of my paper, his judgment still dominated my sense of worth as a learner.

Sixteen years later I neared completion of my doctoral dissertation. My dissertation advisor wrote and rewrote sections of my chapters. I tried to follow his style and failed. One day he suggested that I take an English course; it might help my writing. I visualized Dr. Wrenn nodding in agreement. The next day I received an acceptance from *Elementary English* for my first article. "How much did they change?" my advisor asked. "Hardly anything," I replied.

Buoyed by the news, I asked my advisor if I could write the final chapters without submitting them to him for rewrites. He agreed reluctantly. I completed the dissertation in a week's time. The acceptance of my article and the chance to write without editing helped me begin to find my own voice.

The children I worked with in my dissertation research helped. Each day for four months I sat next to children and observed them writing. The range of their problem-solving strategies and the fact that they'd write without teacher assignments astonished me. I knew I was the first researcher who actually observed children in the process of writing. Children didn't do what the textbooks said they did, and I began to write about them with some authority, to know how I could write so that I sounded like the person I wanted to be. I still didn't know how to help others write.

Don Murray, now professor emeritus of the University of New Hampshire, showed me how to help others in the way he helped me with my own writing (see "The Voice Coach"). Murray has an ear for a writer's voice (as well as a nose for garbage), and his economy of response is remarkable. He'll pick up an article I've struggled with for weeks, read it with the speed of light, and make one comment, "The piece begins over here on page four; that's where your authority is and where you sound like you." Murray doesn't concern himself with the details of sentence structure and language until the final moments in the life of a paper—just the reverse of my own preparation. For the first time I had an alternative to my Bates professor. I began to help others as Murray had helped me.

"Help the writer to teach you about the subject," counseled Murray. "They are the experts. It's up to them to do the speaking and teaching. When I have conferences with my students, they do all the talking." A group of us didn't believe him and videotaped his conferences. His students not only spoke first, they spoke at length.

I knew Murray's approach worked for me, and I began to use it with my students. I used his words—but I still didn't listen to the students. Within three minutes I "knew" what was best for their papers. Keeping quiet while graduate students spoke was difficult. Children were easier to listen to than adults. I listened better as a researcher than as a professor because if I didn't shut up, I recorded no data. The children helped me to help my university students. I began to listen to master's students as a researcher, learning the details of their personal and professional experiences.

About this time I began to understand my Bates experience in a different light. If Dr. Wrenn had only conferred with me about my Tolstoy paper, listened to my concerns about conscientious objection, even challenged me, I might have understood my subject. (I might not have joined the Coast Guard.) Writing would have been a force for learning in my life. Revisiting my experience of failure in college made me bend to the task of helping my students. It strongly influenced my writing, publishing, and teaching. I wrote with the students in class. By switching roles, student-professor, professor-student, I began to experience both sides of the teaching-learning equation. I began to listen more carefully, to find out what they knew. I looked for passion and pressed them for details to help them understand what they cared about. Until I had an alternative to the teaching in my English class at Bates, I couldn't use the incident to help others write and teach themselves.

Although I have told the story of my senior year at Bates many times over the last forty years, it is only within the last ten that I have been able to use it to help others. I've built a career around that encounter with my college professor. At first, the experience moved me to study night and day, then to avoid any possibility of rejection by applying to medical school or graduate studies in Russian. For years I went numb at the prospect of any criticism of my writing. Now I welcome my editor's wise counsel at the line level and praise the heavens that such people exist. I realize that an editor is a valued friend who also respects my knowledge of the subject. "If this is what you mean," my editor writes, "maybe you should construct the passage in this manner."

By studying children's writing I've learned that when a writer works hard to establish new authority, errors abound. My writing at Bates was loaded with errors of logic and language as I struggled to come to terms with death and killing. The content took priority.

I deliberately look for students who struggle to make statements with conviction. I want to meet them in conference and learn what they know about their subject. I listen to their voices; above all, I try to reflect their voices back to them. My first move is to push them for details that show their position more clearly. I remember my first conference with Linda Rief, now a well-published middle school teacher, who was writing about driving her husband's Mercedes to the Durham dump and feeling the car slip backward into the garbage. As she began to tell me the details of the incident, her voice became more and more animated. I was able to begin to help her in the act of composing the way I wish I had been helped on my Tolstoy paper. It took another ten years for me to learn how to refine this approach with others.

Writing this piece has helped me to understand the power of failure and the lasting effects of a voice denied. At the same time I realize the lasting quality of the excellent classical education I received at Bates. Although my professor's remarks still rile me, I was fortunate enough to recover my footing, heal, and go on. I've learned through many workshops with teachers that my college experience of failure was hardly unique. Dr. Wrenn's practices can be multiplied a millionfold. English department professors can be masters of the cynical remark, the well-phrased put-down.

I picked up speed with my research and publishing. I went after bigger questions. Thanks to Donald Murray I knew what it was to find my voice, and I determined to help others find theirs. I couldn't fully recover from my Bates failure until I had passed along what I experienced myself. I wrote the entire *Reading/Writing Teacher's Companion* series based on the premise that we must acquire a sense of our own voice before we try to help our students. When teachers have voices that respect the voices of their students, the quality of writing improves.

Failure is a great teacher. We need to be well acquainted with the stories in which we have not succeeded. They influence our lives as learners and teachers as much as the successful ones. We need to examine these stories again and again, if only because our understanding changes as we grow older. Sometimes failure can do more to help us as learners than success. The wonderful part about stories is the memory they hold. They allow us to redefine ourselves amid complex events.

I have shaped a career from the one comment on my senior paper, "Please change your typewriter ribbon." I was determined that no student of mine would ever go through such a horrendous experience. With the retelling, however, I also realize that the paper had real weaknesses and that the typewriter ribbon was woefully faint. I can shift my point of view and see the incident through Dr. Wrenn's eyes.

TRY THIS: Think back to a failed course, a botched paper, an academic misunderstanding, or a time in which you simply did not come up to your own expectations. Choose one event and shape it into a story. A good story is one you may have told yourself or others again and again.

Cave Man

Psychiatrists like to remind us that a predator sits comfortably within our psyches. Peel off enough of our socialized layers and it will emerge—growling.

Part of my basic training in the U.S. Coast Guard required me to learn to fire the M1 rifle and the .45 automatic pistol, and to learn judo. Killing seemed quite distant when firing weapons—the rifle targets were two hundred yards away—but learning how to kill with our bare hands was another matter. I was both surprised and frightened at the prospect. In our small New England town it was illegal even to take a poke at someone. Now I was going to learn how to defend myself to the death with my bare hands.

For most of my life, especially in elementary school, I was smaller than all my classmates. When the physical education instructor had us line up from tallest to shortest to choose teams, I was always the last in line. I didn't begin to grow until my sophomore year in high school, and I even grew three inches during my first year in college. Someone once said that people who acquire their height later in life will always view themselves as smaller than others. I didn't have an aggressive personality. When I got picked on, I'd fight, but I'd usually lose. How I wished I could be big enough to defend myself more successfully.

When our judo classes began and I deftly learned body slams and how to kill with a chop of the hand, I was surprised to discover mixed feelings of terror and enjoyment, mostly enjoyment. Our instructor, who held a black belt, was also the assistant football coach—tall and heavy, but fast. He demonstrated moves with another instructor much smaller than himself. The small man swung at the instructor, who caught his arm and slammed him to the canvas. I looked for a broken back but the small man jumped to his feet, caught the arm of his partner, and slammed him to the mat. Back and forth they went, trying one maneuver after another, all usually ending with a slam on the mat.

"Okay, now you try it, simple hip roll and slam." We wondered if we'd do permanent damage to each other. We moved into pairs and tried it, including the four-point landing on the mat. I was surprised at how much the four points absorbed the force of the slam and how easy it was to swing your partner and slam him to the mat. Soon the sound of slams echoed throughout the gym. In the barracks within days of training, "make a move" meant an arm shot out to hit a partner or grab someone from behind. Move, countermove, grab, swing, *slam*!

Our egos expanded. Forty male veterans of the playground wars felt their testosterone levels increase with each slam, move, and countermove. Our instructor demonstrated further defensive moves for knives and guns with various "come-along" grips, which allowed you to move a prisoner without benefit of handcuffs. We also learned how to secure an enemy by criss-crossing the man's legs around a pole. If the man fell over, his back would break.

I couldn't wait to get home to demonstrate my skills.

Late in the fall at the end of our basic training at Cape May, New Jersey, I went back to Bates College to visit with friends and former roommates. This was my first time back on campus since graduation the previous spring. We got to chatting about the military. I was looking for an excuse to talk about the Coast Guard. In particular, I was hoping our discussion would lead us toward a judo demonstration.

Two of my closest friends, Swede Anderson and Gordon Hall, seemed to be interested in judo. I recounted how we were taught and my fascination at how easy it was to kill someone. "Here Swede, give a push on my chest. Honest, I won't do anything. I'll just show you a quick hold." Swede pushed on my chest and with a swift move of my two hands I brought him to his knees. Next I demonstrated a come-along grip.

"Want another?" I then demonstrated the simple come-along in which the wrist is turned in the opposite direction against the body, a technique familiar to Military Police. The group soon wanted my full repertoire. Encouraged by their interest, I wanted to lead up to the body slam, the most dramatic of the moves.

I said to Gordon, "Make a move at me, any move." I casually but alertly placed myself in front of him. Gordon made a swift move with his left hand. I stood there immobile, completely surprised. For some reason I'd never encountered anyone who moved first with his left hand. I could only laugh nervously, "Ah, how about coming at me with your right hand? I only know how to do this with righthanders."

It was an important lesson. No matter how well prepared we are for the inevitable, there is always some left-handed move waiting to embarrass us. I can't remember if Gordon was left-handed or if he somehow knew I couldn't handle a move from that direction.

This story may produce other stories about the predator within or about learning itself. I suspect that my inner predator provoked me to pursue the blue shark. There are times when we feel like victims, beat upon in childhood, or when we feel the extremes of inferiority. We've been on the bottom of the pile and we suddenly break out and attack. We need to be acquainted with these stories.

The part of the story I use most is my showdown with Gordon. "Make a move," I challenge, but he comes at me with his left hand. We prepare to teach or learn and our adversaries come at us with the left hand and we don't know what to do. In most teaching/learning situations, as in judo, we need to know what to do next.

TRY THIS: Think of an incident with a student or one of your children, or any learning situation in which you've been totally surprised by someone's action. The next move depended on you. You were or were not successful. Tell that story.

The Test

I presented Betty Lewis with a diamond ring in the Arnold Arboretum in Jamaica Plain, Massachusetts, on June 2, 1953. Her mother and father had become engaged in the same idyllic location twenty-five years before. I thought I'd keep the tradition going.

I assumed that presenting Betty with a ring would mark the end of a year's examination by her family. There were many informal tests, such as driving her father's car and backing it down their long driveway on a hill. Her father wondered how I handled traffic. Was I erratic, steady, or impulsive, or was I sensitive to the vehicle itself? Another informal test was a hike up Tumbledown Mountain in western Maine. Betty warned me that potential suitors to the Lewis clan were observed carefully while climbing. If they could handle a mountain, then maybe the courtship might proceed. Betty informed me that one young man from the city grew weary of the hike and became petulant while slapping blackflies and generally complained about the day. That was the last time the family ever saw that suitor. The young Lewis woman didn't have to be told that he'd never fit in.

I thought I'd passed my tests with flying colors. Betty's mother and father seemed to be pleased that I'd be their future son-in-law. But I hadn't reckoned on Grandpa Ernest Lewis, who thought there was more to the inquisition than a few informal observations.

Ernest was eighty years of age and ruler of the Lewis clan. He'd been a blacksmith most of his life and could fix anything from a broken axle to a wringer-driven washing machine. Ernest was custodian of the gold-headed walking stick given by the defunct *Boston Post* to the oldest man living in Sidney,

Maine. Ernest kept the cane until he died at the age of 106 in 1980. Betty was the first Lewis in the next generation to be engaged. Ernest wanted to be sure I was worthy of the honor of marrying her.

Betty was completing her affiliation as a public health nurse by working in rural Maine out of the Augusta Public Health office. She was staying with her grandparents, Ernest and Mary. I was in the U.S. Coast Guard and hitched to Maine from Boston every weekend I had liberty. The Lewises let me bunk in her aunt's trailer. I'd work to be worthy of my keep. Ernest chose my chores.

Fortunately, I'd had enough training with my Uncle Horatio Nelson Wilbur to know what it was like to be on trial Downeast style. Grandpa greeted me right after breakfast. "Don, those cussed crows are eating my corn as fast as I get it in the ground. The minute I come up to the house they fly in from that tall stand 'a pine and eat away. Now, you do something about it. Come with me." We left the kitchen for the path to the main barn and haymow. "Up here I've got an old double-barreled shotgun. Here are some shells, now get busy."

"I've never fired one of those before, Grandpa. How do you do it?" I wasn't about to pretend what I didn't know. (First on the Downeast list of cardinal sins is pretended knowledge.)

Grandpa cast a sidelong glance, the kind of cocked-head look a poker player gives when he has a full house and he is sure his opponent has only a pair. He cradled the shotgun and scooped some cartridges from a box. "Watch. Nothing to it. Pop two of these in here, and release this safety when you're ready to fire."

"I'll do what I can, Grandpa." I put ten to a dozen cartridges in my pocket and walked toward his garden, down a short slope from the main house and barn.

I heard "Go get 'em, Don" followed by a hoarse chuckle as I walked down the path. I knew Grandpa thought I had little chance of downing any crows. He figured he'd set up a no-win situation. He wanted to see how I handled impossible tasks. I suspect he thought it was even more difficult when I told him I'd never fired a shotgun.

I didn't know anything about shotguns but I did know something about crows. I'd been a bird-watcher most of my life. I didn't like the idea of killing crows but I did want some respect in the family, especially from Grandpa. I had to show my mettle if I was to have a long-term happy life in the clan. Downeasters aren't likely to forget critical moments in early relationships.

I could see the crows pecking at the soil where the corn was newly planted. They soon spotted me and flapped to a tall stand of pine edging the meadow. They posted a lookout in the tallest pine; the rest nestled in the lower branches waiting for me to leave. Grandpa soon followed and went about planting more corn.

I decided to hike a quarter mile north, work my way down the lakeshore, and come in behind the crows while they still faced the garden. A frontal assault would never do. They'd simply fly off to some other tall trees just out of range.

As I hiked to the north, my gun cast professionally over my shoulder like the hunters I'd seen in *Field and Stream,* I was pleased to see that the crows still held their station in the tall pines. It took me another twenty minutes to reach the lake, work the shore, and head back to the pines facing the garden. The air was still, but I could hear the crows cackling their anticipation for another raid on the garden. My steps were noiseless as I stole through the heavy pine needles toward them.

I figured the best I'd get would be one shot before the crows flew off to another location. I popped from tree base to tree base. The crows continued to cackle, oblivious to my approach. About thirty feet from the edge of the wood I looked up to sight on the crows. I was surprised to see three crows sitting on the same limb, not six inches between them.

I remember my dad telling me about the kick of a shotgun when he hunted as a boy, how he'd bounced back from a standing to a sitting position while he nursed a fat lip. I steadied the gun against the side of a pine, sighted down the barrel the way I'd learned to shoot an M1 in basic training, and pulled both triggers. The gun roared and three crows pinwheeled their way to the ground. Two were killed instantly, the other I had to hit over the head. I felt bad about killing the crows but elated about fulfilling my assignment.

With my left hand I picked the crows up by the feet, put the gun over my right shoulder, and strode out of the woods across the field toward the garden. Grandpa was hoeing with his head down, knowing full well I was approaching. Failure would be greeted with a quick glance and chuckle, success with a "well, that's what you were supposed to do" glance, no more.

"Got three crows, Grandpa. What do you want to do with them?"

"Well, you can truss one crow for each of the corners of the garden, but that leaves one post empty, so you'll have to go back and get another 'un." Grandpa dismissed me by turning away to his hoeing. I went back to the trees again and got two more crows.

Twenty-six years later, Grandpa was 106 and sitting in his nursing home wheelchair. He couldn't see, and his hearing was so poor that a microphone sat in his lap so that your voice would be amplified. Betty and I advanced toward his side for a visit. Betty spoke first, "We're here, Grandpa. It's Betty."

"Who?"

"Betty."

"Who?"

"Betty, Grandpa. Your son, Charles's second daughter, Betty."

Grandpa shook his head not understanding. I took the microphone from her hand and spoke. "It's Don, Grandpa. I'm here."

A broad grin swept across his face and his eyes twinkled, "Did ya tell the crows you was a-comin'?"

Cultures often have tests for admitting strangers. Nowhere is this more apparent than when a new member joins a family through marriage. Older generations tend to assume the role of watchdog, applying traditional tests from their forebears.

I was close enough to Grandpa's culture to realize the kind of test in which I was involved. It was more in the line of "what kind of man have we got here?" than an airtight acceptance or rejection of me as his granddaughter's husband. I'd already heard enough muttering about various individuals who had married into the family to know that I'd better come through. I'd never hear the stories the family told about me, yet I knew I should create some good ones for them to pass around.

My Uncle Nelson's little stories and tests were helpful in preparing me for the test of the crows. I was aware that the old Yankee approach to appraising strangers was to observe how well they handled failure. What I didn't include in the crow story was that Grandpa continued my testing the next morning. He asked me to plow some ground with a single-furrowed steel plow while he handled the horse. I'd never done that before and failed miserably, because when the plow hit a rock I couldn't keep the tip in the ground. I'd get a four-foot stretch without a furrow while the horse kept going. Grandpa laughed and I laughed with him. Thus ended my lesson.

TRY THIS: Try to recall an informal test that required you to demonstrate your learning or your ability to handle failure. Perhaps the test was a cultural one in which you knew you were being observed for admission into a group.

The Custodian

In 1958 I became principal of The East Fairhaven School, the very building I had taught in for two years. I didn't know much about being a principal and even less about what went on in everyday building activity. Lee Rose, our droll custodian, who hated to see Friday come because it meant Monday was only two days away, got me through that first year with quiet humor and a savvy sense of what kids were about.

Why wouldn't a custodian, who had to clean up after kids every day, know their habits better than anyone else in the building? Lee, an old Navy man with gray hair who often wore dark green work clothes, watched children on the playground before, during, and after school. He cleaned up messes in lavatories, the papers they dropped in the corridors while they waited for the bus, and the food they left in the cafeteria. These same children picked putty from newly glazed windows, turned wheels that ought to have been left alone, disturbed water bubblers, and jumped doors off their hinges in the lavatories, all in the normal process of being kids. Lee didn't complain, he just watched and knew when events took a serious turn.

Three weeks into my principalship he met me as I came in the door on a Thursday morning. "Don, we've got troubles. Four banks of windows are smashed on the playground side of the new addition."

Right away I knew I was being tested as the new principal. I'd succeeded Helen Porter, a dynamic and experienced administrator, who engendered much pride in the building. I couldn't recall any incident in the previous two years that paralleled this one. I could hear the voices, "Graves can't hack it. Bring back Helen Porter."

"Got any hunches, Lee?"

"I'll think on it and get back to you."

About recess time Lee shuffled into my office. "I think I know who did it. Day before yesterday I saw some of the New Boston Road boys fooling around on the playground after school. See, I left about four-thirty yesterday afternoon and no one was on the playground. Now it had to be walkers, 'cuz all the buses had gone and no kid is going to come two miles back to the school to play. I figure it's got to be some of those tough kids down the road. Couldn't be nobody else. You call in Walter. Walter can help you."

Lee not only gave the full diagnosis but he knew who would spill the story about what had happened. Walter, a third grader, was the weak link in the New Boston Road group. I called him into my office. "Walter, why did you break those windows on the new addition?"

Walter, a boy with tousled blond hair, thin of build and short of stature, whined, "I didn't do it, but I know who did." Case solved. Later, three boys confessed to the smashing.

About a month later Lee stood silently in my office waiting for me to finish my conference with a parent. When I saw Lee waiting I knew he had important news. He usually handled most problems by himself. When he came to see me I knew I'd better listen. Besides, as a new principal, I was receiving an education no university could teach.

"Don, this may not amount to anything, but it could. Thought you'd better know. I don't know how he does it, but one of the boys is able to turn off the water in the boys' lavatory. There is a wheel about twelve feet up that turns off a valve that supplies the water to the urinals. I have to get a ten-foot stepladder to turn it back on." Lee shook his head, partly in admiration for the child's ingenuity, partly in worry about what might happen if there was no water.

"What do you figure we need to do, Lee? Any ideas?" I said, trusting his usual understanding of such matters.

"Nope. I'll just have to wait and hope he doesn't do it again. I guess the thing I worry about most is, suppose the kid who climbs up there falls and hits that concrete floor?"

I hadn't thought about the boy getting hurt. My immediate reaction was to the problem of no water in the urinals. I hadn't yet become a principal who thought children first, building second.

"My God, I hadn't thought about that, Lee." I knew he couldn't put up a sign, "Don't touch the valve or wheel." That would be an open invitation to every other boy in the school.

Lee turned to go, his face placid as usual. "I'll think on it."

Anxious about what might happen I sought Lee out each morning. "Valve still on? Had any ideas about what to do?"

"Nope, still workin' on it."

The following week the valve was turned off again. For the first time since I'd worked at the school, I saw Lee in an agitated state. "Don, we've got to do something. I've got an idea, but you'll have to help. Get me one of those ditto carbons. You know, the carbon part of the master. I'll rub that purple stuff all over the valve wheel so that when it's turned off, the boy's hands will be covered with the stuff. You game for that?"

"I sure am, Lee. Put it on the wheel and the minute the valve is turned off we'll check all the hands. Where did you ever come up with that one?"

"I don't know. I just kept thinkin' on it. That's all. I was throwing out the trash in the ditto room the other day and saw that carbon sheet. Got some on my hands and then it struck me we could use some of that on the wheel and catch our phantom."

About a week later Lee stood in my office grinning from ear to ear, far more than his usual laconic manner permitted. "The valve is off, Don. Let's go find him."

I decided to start with the upper grades and move down. We asked each of the boys to present his hands. We found nothing in the sixth or fifth grades. In the fourth grade one of the boys presented a hand all covered in purple ditto ink.

"Well, Michael," I said. "How did you get that purple on your hands?"

"Oh, I was fooling around on the playground. There's some stuff out there."

"Michael," I said, adding seriousness to my tone, "that purple comes from ink like this." I took the ditto paper and rubbed some of the blue on his hands to match the color already there. "Michael, how did you manage to climb up and turn off the wheel of the valve in the boy's lavatory?"

Michael looked puzzled, as if he couldn't believe we knew. He continued to study our faces while saying nothing. "Come down to the office, Michael, and tell me how you did it."

Two boys had given Michael a boost for a toehold on the wall. Michael was small, part natural gymnast and part adventurer. He hadn't realized that the valve turned off the water in the lavatory. He was more interested in proving to the other boys that he could scale the wall to the ceiling. Turning the valve was proof that he'd succeeded in climbing so high.

As Michael sat and talked in my office, I could see Lee Rose standing at the counter talking with my secretary, Emily. I knew he could hear our conversation. As usual he was quiet, picking up information from Michael. He never knew when he might need evidence for the next conundrum the children would present.

Wherever we work there are people whose positions allow them to see and know things we can never know. We need to open the doors that will enable us to learn from them. Of course, I didn't know how important that process was when I first became principal. Desperation is often the best teacher.

Every day Lee Rose cleaned, hauled papers, and checked the operation of sinks, toilets, boilers, and equipment in the cafeteria. He observed the habits of children as they affected his work. He was well acquainted with their ingenuity. He cared about their welfare and saw dangers I could never observe.

TRY THIS: Consider your responsibility where you teach or work. Think about the knowledge possessed by people who work with you and tell or write a story in which you learned from them in an entirely unexpected way.

Graves vs. the Town of Fairhaven

Five months after I was appointed school principal, my younger brother George sued my employer, the town of Fairhaven, Massachusetts. The morning after town meeting my brother called me. "Did you see what the town did yesterday? They cut the school budget."

"I know. So what. They've cut the school budget at town meeting for the last twenty-five years."

"It's against the law. I won't let them get away with it."

"What are you going to do then?"

"Sue 'em." George wasn't a lawyer, he was a newly appointed teller at the Fairhaven Institution for Savings. Banks didn't like employees who sued the town in which they worked. It was bad for business. I was fast with words, George with action.

When I was nine and George seven, we had a small skiff that three big boys took away from us. In the face of such odds I stood back and watched. But George approached the biggest of the three at the end of the pier. "You can't have the boat."

"You gonna' stop me, you little twerp?" The boy, a full head and a half taller, made mocking feints and jabs around George, who was standing with his arms at his side. From my position I couldn't see the punch, but I heard the muffled thump as George buried his fist in the boy's stomach. The boy staggered backward, lost his balance, and landed shouting in the shallow water of the creek. Before the other two boys could react George was off and running.

Ten years later George was the youngest boy to enter Bill McGowan's professional baseball umpire's school in the Grapefruit League in Florida. The kid, as he was called, umpired Triple-A minor league baseball. Most of the umpires had

68

gray hair or bald spots, some mark of maturity to back their decisions. George had a brush cut, sharp eyes, and a keen sense of justice.

When he came north and umpired in New England I remember seeing him catch a bang-bang double play, covering second base and, with a quick pivot and sprint, calling the runner out at first. A posse of athletes and coaches rushed from the dugout and surrounded George, who stood with arms folded, face immobile. After several minutes of arguing "safe," the group dispersed still muttering. George had said nothing.

After the game I asked, "How could you be so sure you were right on that first base call? Don't you ever wonder if you were wrong?"

"Nope. You have to position yourself to see, then listen for the sound of the ball in the glove and the foot on the base. Whichever comes first determines the call." At the time I was a second-year English major, carefully trained in the liberal arts tradition that nothing was ever all right or all wrong.

Ten years later, George was suing the town of Fairhaven for cutting the school budget. We both had the same education at the family breakfast table. Dad was a superintendent of schools who had mentioned more than once that school boards were agents of the state. What the boards adopted was law. Unless they acted unreasonably their decisions should go unchallenged. George owned a small summer cottage in the town. As a taxpayer he could take action. Within a day he had signatures from nine other taxpayers and a school lawyer, Bill O'Keefe from Boston College.

George sued the town he loved. He was an all-star basketball player who guided his team to the New England Class-B championship. The town raised money to send the team to New York City for a weekend of the NCAA basketball championships. When his apartment burned, the town held a benefit basketball game to raise funds for his family. But George's was a lover's quarrel. The town he loved ought to provide a decent education for its children.

George brought suit in February 1959. The case didn't come before the Superior Court until March 1960. Meanwhile, in February 1960, the town again cut the school budget. George sued the town a second time. The judge found in favor of Graves and the petitioners, but the town appealed to the State Supreme Court. In January 1961 the Supreme Court ruled in favor of Graves and the petitioners on the first case. The cuts were restored and the town was fined by the Court. In February 1961 the finance committee met in public and again discussed proposed cuts to the school budget. George called the judge and an agent of the court appeared announcing that anyone speaking for cuts would be held in contempt of court.

A year later George ran for a seat on the school board. The town that knew a love-hate relationship with "the kid" voted him into office with a landslide victory. He served three terms on the board and two terms as chair. He retired as a school board member at the age of thirty-five. The bank that worried about George's suit eventually promoted him to vice-president.

I always felt slow next to my "little" brother, George. He had a short fuse and reacted quickly to issues of injustice, exploding on the spot and moving quickly to action. I exploded—but not until the middle of the night or several weeks later, when it was too late to do anything about the matter. Sometimes I think my delay was connected to an inordinate desire to keep the peace. I wanted to be friends with everyone, and friendship in the face of unjust situations needed some rethinking. I've always admired George's ability to react. On the other hand, George admires my ability to write and think long-term, to hold back and not react so quickly.

There are stories we tell that define us in relation to our brothers and sisters. These are lifetime stories that govern our lives and our relations with other people.

TRY THIS: Think of a situation in which your behavior can be defined as distinct from a brother or sister. Tell a story about an occurrence that exemplifies the differences between you. If you had no siblings, choose a friend and do the same. Does your story carry over to your understanding of yourself in relation to others? Discuss.

The Preacher

I didn't really believe that athletes could be Christians. In my mind there was too great a distance between the preachers I knew and the athletes I'd seen perform in college and professional sports. An athlete I much respected, Bart Leach, who was all-Ivy and second team All-American in basketball, invited me to attend a meeting of the Fellowship of Christian Athletes. Bart was a local hero in our small town of Fairhaven, Massachusetts, and a close friend of my brother's. I'd always been curious about his faith, so when he invited us to the meeting I went to view and meet professional athletes. Sports in our family was closer to our true religion than anything I'd encountered in church. At thirty years of age I was a school principal and had done some coaching. I was restless about the direction of my life.

A man named Gary Demarest strode briskly to the Springfield College stage and said, "Well, as the mummy once said, 'I'm a little pressed for time.' " The audience of college coaches and athletes groaned. Demarest was from California and fit my New England image of a west coast athlete: curly blond hair with high cheekbones, a rugged six feet, two inches tall. I imagined he was either a surfer or a beach volleyball addict. He certainly didn't fit my image of a Christian. Demarest quickly followed with a Bob Hope–type monologue. "Yes, my mother and father are in the iron and steel business; my mother irons and my father steals." The audience warmed to his humor. Used to staid New England preachers, I was caught off guard by his jokes and antics.

Just as I got used to his humor he shifted gears to introduce the main speaker, President Olds of Springfield College. "President Olds is one of the youngest and most brilliant college presidents in the U.S. today. He has published much in the field of philosophy, is an athlete, former boxer, and now college president . . . Greet President Olds."

I went to meet the college and professional athletes but left impressed by Gary Demarest and his power and ability to talk to athletes from the stage. I, like others, enjoyed his sense of play and quick ability to move to deeper subjects. I remember thinking, "I want to believe what this guy believes. When he speaks to the crowd I feel as though he is speaking directly to me."

A year later I was in charge of a sports banquet and brought Gary and Otto Graham, the quarterback of the Cleveland Browns, in as speakers. I drove Gary back to the airport in Boston. Enroute he asked if I would be the new Director of Christian Education in Hamburg, New York, where he was about to become minister. I accepted. Gary's request came at a time in my life when I wanted to be near someone who stood for ideals I could grow into. Two months later I left my job as school principal and arrived with my family of six to take up my new position.

I began my apprenticeship as a minister of education without any seminary study, yet I soon was preaching, hospital calling, and teaching. Gary introduced me to the congregation: "And now Don Graves. I know you have all been waiting to meet him, for the excitement has been building since our first meeting back in May [it is now July]. The word is out; he is a true professional. The tradition of the church has always been to bring in someone fresh from seminary. We believe we have a committed Christian and a superior educator in Don Graves, who is one of the leading young educators in the State of Massachusetts." To my mind his statement was pure fiction, but fiction or not, I felt I had to reach some level of excellence to live up to it. I admired Gary and didn't want to disappoint him.

Gary Demarest never gave me any formal lessons in speaking or preaching. In fact, I can't recall a single discussion about how to preach. I simply observed what he did and tried to follow. I learned to speak in about the same way I might learn to play tennis. Someone once said, "Want to improve your game, tennis or golf, anything? Play with an expert."

Gary Demarest spoke from the pulpit with easy power. He mixed the conversational with the narrative, evoked humor in the details of our common human predicament, then nailed his main point home with strong declarative sentences based in scripture.

His first sermons were based on John: "That which was from the beginning, which we have heard, which we have seen with our eyes, which we have looked upon and touched with our hands, concerning the word of life." These are the Jewish proofs for authenticating experience, in this case, for the Messiah. When Gary spoke, he delivered his words clearly and with the voice of authority. There was no wavering, no "it seems to me." I dreamed of the day when I could deliver words in that manner.

In his opening sentences he'd usually hint that he'd just learned something in his study of scripture that would be very useful to us today. Thus he implied that the rest of the sermon would be a journey of learning that we would take with him. I remember thinking, "At every point there is an expectation that something is about to happen." There is a saying that writers often use: "No surprise for the writer, then no surprise for the reader." The same could apply to Gary Demarest's sermon preparations: "No surprise for the preacher, then no surprise for the congregation."

My greatest speaking challenge was not in preaching from the pulpit but in conducting our early morning Bible study. Every Wednesday morning we held two Bible studies, one at six forty-five for people who went to work, and one at ten for retired people, those off-shift, and mothers at home with children. The sessions were very well attended with about 150 at the early one and 200 at the later one. Holding a Bible in his hand, Gary taught scripture nonstop for the full hour time slot. Once again, his speaking was effortless, conversational, and filled with good humor and wisdom.

"Oh Don," he said one day, "I've got to be out of town in three weeks. I'd like you to take the Bible study. You'll have the thirteenth chapter of 1 Corinthians. I'm very sorry to be away. That's one of my favorite chapters." My heart sank. New and with no seminary background or previous depth in scripture study, even as a lay person, I set out to prepare.

Above all, I didn't want the quality of our sessions to drop just because I was the teacher. When I stood up to teach I wanted to be casual yet authoritative, at the least to "look good."

I was relieved to find that the thirteenth chapter was short, only thirteen verses. I immediately memorized them so that I could think about them no matter what I was doing. I picked up two Bible commentaries, then studied the essential Greek, especially *agape*, the Greek word for love as the apostle Paul redefined it—love with no strings attached—the word used to show God's love for us.

A combination of Gary's example and the pure terror of my lack of background pushed me to work four or five hours a day for the three weeks prior to my presentation. In one sense I was trying rather foolishly to be Gary Demarest, the senior pastor, as I conducted the class. As false as the situation may have been, I certainly learned. I have a hunch that there has to be a perceived gap between a mentor's ability and the person trying to learn, something to which the learner consciously aspires.

I deliberately spoke without notes. In fact, I spoke without a Bible in my hands, since I'd memorized those thirteen short verses. The frame of scripture was given to me. I merely nailed my narratives and commentaries plus background to fill the slots demanded by each of the verses. Best of all, new insights about the scriptures came to me during the class. I'd just begun to experience the surprise element in teaching. The frame of memorization and the discipline of extensive preparation became a foundation for discovery and surprise. In successive Bible studies and in other teaching in the church, I focused much more on what I'd learned about the class and made the Bible study more of a dialogue between us.

After that first class I watched Gary carefully for new angles to apply to my own teaching. I could never match his humor but I could at least see that humor came from the most ordinary of human foibles, usually our attempts to be more than we are. I realized that I needed to collect more stories about people in everyday life and hunt for larger meaning in the more mundane situations in life.

Only recently have I begun to appreciate what I learned from Gary in the two years we worked together. I certainly learned the meaning of discipline and study as necessary underpinnings to spontaneity. Commitment and conviction, the voice with which the speaker reaches out to the audience, are also based in sound study and discipline.

I'm struggling to pinpoint one final element of Gary's preaching and teaching, something he did that made the congregation or group he was addressing aware of their own power. He used humor to bring an audience together. I'd see people anticipating his humor and poking each other in agreement. That's one level, but somehow the group also has to feel they can do things together. They walk into church as individuals but leave as a community ready for action. Sometimes he used stories to show how the Holy Spirit filled the disciples with power or how different groups in trouble became forces for the good. The implication was always very clear: you too can be that force. Try it and find out.

Gary Demarest gave me the basic fundamentals for developing my approach to speaking and I have continued to experiment. In talks away from the pulpit, for example, Gary allowed nothing to stand between himself and the audience. At the time I didn't understand his reasoning, but now I realize that the audience benefits from seeing the whole person: arms, legs, posture are all means to communicating a message. It also creates a more intimate connection: "He is speaking directly to me."

I've also come to understand that the distance between the speaker and the front row is very important. Before any talk begins an unspoken question exists in the minds of the audience: "Who does this person [the speaker] think we are?" I approach the question in two ways. First, I always arrive early to chat with the audience I'll be addressing. I need to get to know them, find out why they came and what's on their minds professionally. Above all, I want the audience to see me speaking to them before the talk. Second, I begin conversationally, either through humor or a well-chosen story. This helps the audience to get to know each other. I've learned that audiences listen to each other react to the talk as much as they listen to the speaker. The closer to the audience the speaker is, the more the nearness communicates "I'd like to get to know you."

This is the power of the effective mentor: we continue to draw on their presence many years later. Their real influence, however, is in our continued transformation of ourselves. Their demonstrations were so powerful, we wished to experiment on our own.

TRY THIS: Try to recall mentors from whom you have learned and an instance of direct instruction or demonstrated example. What did you learn from them that you still use today? How do you continue to refine your early learning?

A Royal Adventure

I filed into my first class at Union Seminary in New York City in July 1963. It was a graduate seminar on the Sermon on the Mount in the gospel of Matthew. I looked left and right trying to size up my peers. These were not young men and women. Some carried Greek testaments; I didn't know a word of Greek. I was studying in New York because my church conference had recommended it in preparation for ordaination.

The day before, my wife, Betty, had left me and my books and suitcases on the curb in front of Hastings Hall at 122nd Street and Broadway. The deep gong of Riverside Church a block away tolled the quarter hour as I watched Betty head up-town toward the Bronx-Whitestone Bridge. I'd be in New York for eight weeks while she and our four children stayed with my parents on Cape Cod.

A lanky, balding man of about thirty-eight entered the room. He was dressed in an open shirt and wrinkled slacks. I guessed this must be Professor Marcus Barth, son of the famous biblical scholar, Karl Barth. He extended his arms to us as he spoke. "Friends, let us begin. The course is titled 'Sermon on the Mount.' Let us begin this adventure in the scriptures. We do not know where they will take us or how far we will get. But who cares? We will have a royal adventure."

As he spoke I noticed that he had no text, no books of any kind, not even a Bible. What I didn't know was that Marcus Barth knew the entire Bible by heart. Later, classmates who knew him better would say, "Give him any verse in scriptures and he will quote you what comes before and after it." I had never met a man like this.

In a thick German accent he began the lecture: "And seeing

the multitudes. . . ," the first part of the first line of the Sermon on the Mount. The entire two-hour class was devoted to the first half of the first verse.

His eyes danced as he spoke, but this was no ordinary dancing. He had an air of expectation not unlike a magician about to remove the drapery covering an exciting object. All eyes were on Marcus. All eyes were on Marcus' eyes. We couldn't help focusing on his eyes because his poor vision separated him from us by many, many layers of glass. The effect was one of gazing down long tunnels at two dancing black pupils. They danced in appropriate rhythm to his discovery with us of the Sermon on the Mount.

" 'And seeing the multitudes,' " he went on, "do you know who the multitudes were? Our translation does no justice to what Matthew is writing here. In Greek the word for multitude is *orloi*. These were the ordinary commoners, the people who had nothing. Now in Hebrew, and Matthew wrote this in Hebrew, the word is *ame-ha-aretz*. These were the riffraff, the people kicked out of the temple, the lost. You would call them bums. Isn't this exciting? Don't you see what this means? The Sermon on the Mount is for the bums." We chatted back and forth about the meaning of this interpretation.

At the end of class Barth announced that he would like to eat with us in the refectory, not with the faculty in the dining room. He wanted to know us, hear our thinking, listen to our worries and our excitements. I heard later that the faculty were upset that the visiting scholar from Switzerland wasn't engaged with them.

His assignment for the entire course was simple, "Choose one verse and exhaust it. This will be a thorough exegesis that results in a major paper. Take risks, be wild, let the scriptures lead you. Live with it. Memorize it. But above all, let the scriptures lead. Be the servant of scripture. Who knows what excitement will be yours!"

I was captivated by his enthusiasm but terrified at the same time. Unlike the other students, who were seminary graduates, I had not studied Greek or Hebrew. But I was not about to drop the course. The promise of Barth's enthusiasm, inspiration, and energy convinced me I might be able to pull off the assignment. In a way I didn't care. Barth's opening lecture on the first part of the first verse had already turned my thinking upside down.

The second class meeting was packed with students and a multitude of visitors. I arrived twenty minutes early and ended up in the third row.

Barth began again. "And seeing the multitudes, he went up on the mountain, and when he sat down the disciples came to him. And he opened his mouth and taught them, saying . . . blessed are the poor." This is Matthew's way of telling us that the Messiah is here. When a rabbi spoke, it was customary for everyone to stand while the rabbi sat. But this is no ordinary rabbi. When the rabbi sits it is time for everyone else to listen. Notice that the disciples came to him. This is a scene from a royal court. The king sits. The courtiers gather round. But notice that Matthew doesn't simply record "he spoke." Rather, he writes "he opened his mouth." He captures the precise moment of royalty. Everyone is waiting for words from the king. Like a press conference with the president."

"Well, the context is one of a king, the Messiah, offering congratulations. We have few parallels for this in our lives. Today the picture might be one of a lawyer in the presence of bums, the unwashed, who breaks the seal of the will and says, 'Congratulations, you have come into a wonderful inheritance.' The central proclamation of this whole Sermon on the Mount from the Messiah is 'Congratulations, you lucky bums!' "

I have never forgotten the details of those lectures. Barth carried no notes. There is something about a teacher with no notes; in effect, I capture what is part of his oral tradition. I began in that class to sense how scriptures could be passed unwritten from generation to generation. Of course it was more than memorization. The scriptures possessed Barth. We wanted them to possess us. He wanted nothing to stand in the way: no books, notes, or anything else. He wanted us to bet our lives, to take risks on the basis of what we found.

We ate with Barth, debated, laughed, and pressed on with our exegesis. He laughed at himself and showed us the humor in the scriptures. We got off the subject one day discussing the apostle Paul's dictum that women should have their heads covered during worship. "Ah, you have no parallel for this today.

The whores in that society in Corinth were the ones who didn't have their heads covered. A woman coming to worship uncovered, yah, be the same your grandmother come to church in a bikini."

I managed to learn the Greek alphabet, which wasn't too far removed from the Russian alphabet I already knew. Having learned the alphabet, I was able to use the Greek dictionary and also do the word studies in both the Old and New Testaments. Barth convinced us there wasn't anything we wouldn't be able to do.

The night before final exams he noticed how uptight I was. "Graves," he said, "what you need is a good movie with some sex in it. Go watch *Irma La Douce*. Relax. Laugh. That is the best preparation."

I went to the movie. He was right. Such a teacher, in love with scriptures, taking risks, laughing all the way. Serious to the point of being a revolutionary but never taking himself seriously in the process. A royal adventure indeed.

I am always surprised that the details of Marcus Barth's first class remain so clearly in my mind. I even remember the Greek and Hebrew words. What did the man do to produce such retention?

His knowledge of the subject allowed him to speak with no notes, so we could take in a broad range of information, which enhanced the meaning of the text. I could see his entire body, his dancing eyes, the movement of his arms as they interpreted his careful, yet vibrant language. His language was invitational, as if he was sharing what he knew. I felt no fear that I might not remember. Rather, he invited us to extend what he was saying. We were hanging around with a learner, the best kind of teacher.

Of course, it may be that I was more ready to hear his words than I could know then or now. I was ready for the Messiah's declaration of freedom that matched Barth's own teacherly declaration.

TRY THIS: Think of a teaching experience in which you are able to recall the content in precise detail. Tell (or write) that story and then speculate about why you remember so well.

The Pro

"Here's a bucket of balls. Hit 'em." I thought Sam, the golf pro, would start the lesson with a brief lecture on the finer points of driving a golf ball. I'm more comfortable with words. I didn't like the idea of showing how little I knew. I'd only been playing golf for two weeks.

I strode to the tee with a number four driver, placed the golf tee in the ground, and put the ball on it. The pro stood well off the tee area and about twenty-five feet away staring at some golfers coming down the opposite fairway. He seemed as uninterested in their play as he was in mine. Sam didn't fit my image of a golf pro. When I signed up for instruction I imagined a lean, young Jack Nicklaus, broad at the shoulder and narrow at the waist. Sam was heavy in the jowl and thick in the middle with narrow, slitlike eyes that gave him a look of detachment.

I decided to hit the ball with authority. The first time I missed. The second time the ball shanked wide to the fairway leading to the ninth hole. "Try keeping your head down. Just do that." His voice came from the left and behind me.

"All right," I said to myself, "I'll do the first thing he says and if that works maybe I'll listen to the next thing he says." I hit the ball. It didn't go very far but at least it was on the fairway.

"That's it," said Sam. "Keep your head down and keep hittin' 'em." I was hitting the ball steadily now. I didn't mind that Sam was watching. His interest in me seemed to perk up.

"Okay, you're on your way, but let's take a look at your feet." Sam sauntered over and took the club from my hand. "Watch. Get comfortable. You're standing like someone is going to strike you out." Sam put a ball on a tee, spread his feet apart slightly, rocked back and forth to display comfort, and put his head down. Whoosh, the ball shot high, seemed to pick up speed, and bounced on the fairway about 220 yards distant. I had no idea a short, pudgy man could be capable of such ease and power. "Get the idea? Keep hittin' 'em," he tossed back over his shoulder. The ball started to rise a little and move straighter still on the fairway. Again my confidence rose.

Before our session was over, Sam had interrupted me four times to attend to keeping my head down, the placement of my feet and shoulders, my grip, and my follow-through. In two subsequent meetings he attended to a number of further refinements. Thanks to Sam I was able at least to hit a ball off the tee with respectability. I never played golf beyond that spring in 1962, when Sam showed me how to hit a ball. A growing family and the press of work ruled out further play. Sam's skill as a teacher, however, has stayed with me.

I didn't understand how Sam worked as a teacher until twenty years later, when I was teaching a basic course in writing. Sam knew enough about golf to observe fifty things wrong with my approach to hitting a ball in the first five minutes of my lesson. He stood at a distance, giving me some privacy for those first embarrassing moments. He knew that help can only be given in the midst of the process. Discussing the game was irrelevant. I didn't know how to hit the ball and I needed practice. Sam needed to find out how to help me. Fortunately, the thousands of hours he had played the game and the hundreds of golfers he'd helped showed him what to choose first: "Keep your head down and your eye on the ball."

He introduced me to only three or four pointers, carefully sandwiched between bouts of extensive practice. A lecture on my errors, innumerable as they were, would not have straightened my drives. He used few words. He was almost invisible. He placed his confidence in his apt selection of tips. He knew that if I saw something work, he didn't have to say very much.

Good teachers can appear in the most unlikely places; this is especially true if we are looking for good teaching/learning stories. Think of all the good teachers in your life. I believe they have common characteristics:

They allow for abundant practice. They know how to observe. They limit the learning field. They assess well what it is you need to learn. They don't hover.

TRY THIS: Choose your best teacher from a field totally unrelated to your own. Tell the story of how they taught you.

Meet Myrtle

She came in an old 1959 Plymouth station wagon with flying fenders. The rear shocks were canted, and the fenders perforated by the salt of Buffalo roads in winter. The Science Lady, as I shall call her, was as disheveled as her auto. An old brown hat sat on her head as if in absent-minded acknowledgment of social convention when she left her farm for the city. She waved her arms as she directed the unloading of twenty or thirty cartons so stuffed they touched the roof of her car.

I was now director of language and special programs for the city of Lackawanna, New York. I supervised a Saturday morning science workshop and the Science Lady was the instructor. My job was to help her unload and get her things inside the school, set up chairs and desks, perk the coffee, and see that the workshop went smoothly. The front office informed me that the Science Lady was a wonder and could present all the flora, fauna, and phyla from stuffed to live animals, ants, birds, and other creatures. We worked in a city and city teachers and kids needed to see things for themselves rather than gaze at pictures of them in a book.

The only entrance open that early in the morning was through an opening for delivering coal. This meant going down a steel ladder, walking through a cavernous boiler room, up another set of steel-runged stairs, and into the school corridor. The Science Lady barked warnings as each container made its long journey up and down ladders and finally into the school. There were the obvious labelings on each of the boxes: owl, ants, plants. One box was a little heavier than the others. The label read Myrtle. I imagined flowering myrtle in pots.

The Science Lady ordered three large tables for the front of the workshop area. She arranged her classified wares in categories on the tables, placing the empty boxes on the floor beneath them. The rest of the room was arranged in a twenty-five seat amphitheater, with extra tables pushed against the outside windows at the back of the room. Teachers arrived in clumps and drank coffee. Some wandered around the tables inspecting the stuffed snowy owl and the glass-sided ant farm.

Literacy, particularly reading, was the centerpiece of most of the workshops. Working with the actual stuff of science, living or stuffed animals, was new. The Science Lady took us through each of the kingdoms by lecture, manipulation, and classification. Most of the phyla emerged from what was already on table tops. Teachers enjoyed themselves as they sipped coffee, chatted, and asked questions of the workshop leader.

I sensed, however, that the Science Lady was working toward some dramatic crescendo. "I have one more important kingdom we have failed to consider this morning," she barked. "I'd like you to meet Myrtle." As she began to speak, she knelt down and raised a large box to the top of the table. She flipped open the cover, paused, glanced around the room, and announced, "Yes, snakes, a boa constrictor, actually. Meet Myrtle." Gradually, she unwound twelve-foot Myrtle from the box.

I was seated in the first row in front of the tables, about six feet from the Science Lady . . . and Myrtle. From behind me shrieks and screams erupted. I turned and saw open mouths and bulging eyes. Three or four of the women were standing on the rear tables against the windows and two more were in the process of joining them there.

I turned back to look at Myrtle. I refused to follow the script of a screaming human being. As a child I enjoyed playing with the adders and garter snakes that lived in the rocks near our home in Rhode Island. But Myrtle was a twelve-foot boa constrictor. The Science Lady walked toward me. The workshop occurred in 1966, well before the women's movement was under way. I suspect that even then, a cool male in the midst of screaming women was a challenge the Science Lady couldn't resist.

Myrtle was draped over the Science Lady's shoulder on the right side, the tail wound two to three times around her waist. She looked as if she was preparing to play the tuba except the horn part was missing and in its place was a large snake head with a darting tongue. Myrtle's head extended about three feet in front of the Science Lady in my direction. Myrtle's tongue darted her greeting.

My chest grew tighter and my shoulders drew in. I leaned back, and in an attempt to appear confident and casual, blurted, "Uh, I wonder how much she weighs?"

"I'm not really sure," said the Science Lady. "What do you think? Here, I'll let you hold Myrtle, then you tell me." She extended her arms with Myrtle and I rose obediently from my chair. I didn't want to displease the lady with a twelve-foot boa constrictor.

She began by instructing me on how to hold Myrtle. Her directions were simple: "Myrtle gets nervous if she doesn't feel support!" She began to transfer Myrtle to my tense carriage. "Now, place your hands just so, about four feet back from her head. She needs support for her head when she gets curious and extends like she is right now." As I placed my right hand under Myrtle and just back from her head, I heard a sound behind me like water going down a drain, a sort of collective gasp punctuated by "My God, he's going to do it."

The Science Lady then transferred Myrtle over to my shoulder and let her tail wrap around my waist. I felt a stiffening in Myrtle's tail. "Keep your arm up and give her support," barked my first sergeant in science.

I pushed my arm up and Myrtle relaxed her grip on my waist. But Myrtle was fast becoming interested in the people on my left beyond the resources of my right arm. My arm strained. Myrtle's darting-tongue explorations on my left side brought her torso over my right shoulder to just under my chin. More gasps, including my own.

"Use your left hand, Mr. Graves. Myrtle isn't trying to strangle you. She's still looking for support. Now put her head in your left hand, and just pull against her body but away from your neck with your right hand. She needs something to pull against. The pull is support too." Myrtle relaxed and seemed to appreciate my efforts.

About four minutes into this learning episode I recalled my original cue for getting into the mess in the first place. "Uh, I think she weighs about fifty to sixty pounds," I stuttered. "Now, how do I get her off?"

I hardly remember anything the Science Lady taught except for the part about learning to hold the boa constrictor. My idle comment about wondering how much the snake weighed put me in a learning situation I'd just as soon had passed me by.

I think the Science Lady knew my ego wouldn't allow me to say, "Ah, no thanks. You tell me how much the snake weighs." Instead, I did as she directed, concentrating so intently on holding the snake properly that I forgot why Myrtle was draped on me in the first place. I'm still not sure I need to know how to hold a boa constrictor.

TRY THIS: Try to recall an event in which you learned something that may have been unnecessary—that is, your ego led you into a hair-raising situation. Bring out the humorous elements.

A Report to the Arabs

"Don, we've got to do something for the Arabian families. They don't know how well their children are doing," complained Mary Alvira, teacher of the English as a Second Language Program in Lackawanna, New York.

"You're right, Mary. We've got the report cards in Serbo-Croatian, Polish, Spanish, and Italian but I'm not sure where to go for help on the Arabic." I was director of reading and language programs for the city, but I consistently ducked the Arab report card problem. I didn't know any adults in the Arabic-speaking community well enough to commission the report card. Report cards are a sensitive business. In each instance, with the exception of one card written in Spanish, Mary's native language, we were able to double-check report card accuracy with a native speaker.

Report cards recorded information about children's progress in such areas as language use, reading, interactions with other children, vocabulary growth, and independence in using the room. The meaning of each category was explained, and the three columns to the right of each section provided space to check off progress. Even if we didn't know a language we could match the category with the English version and check the appropriate column for strong, good, or slower progress.

The Arab children represented the second largest non-English-speaking group in our program. At that time most of the non-English speakers were attracted by jobs in Lackawanna's Bethlehem Steel Corporation plant, the third largest steel plant in the world. Most of the Arabic-speaking families were from Yemen, one of the poorest countries in the Arab world. In each family's case, a familiar pattern of emigration evolved. First, the father left the country, got a job, and made enough money to send for the eldest son or uncle. When most of the wage-earning males had arrived, the mother came, followed by the daughters. Women were not allowed out of the home unless some had been in the United States long enough to understand local culture. Thus, most of the Arabian children in our program, with the exception of two young women, were male.

Several weeks after Mary's query I dropped in to see Julian Dargan, the director of Friendship House, a community center three doors down from the site of our ESL program at Queen of All Saints School. I told him about our progress in working with the Arabian children, many of whom stopped by Friendship House after school. At the same time I expressed my frustration at not solving the Arab report card problem.

"We may have the solution right here, Don. Did you know that our accountant and business manager, Mr. Hassan, is Lebanese? I believe he is fluent in Arabic."

I had been introduced to Mr. Hassan several times before. He was a stocky, well-dressed businessman in suit and tie. Beyond a pleasant smile, he rarely initiated conversation with others. He quietly worked with budgets and figures in a small office off the main entrance to the settlement house.

"Julian says that you speak Arabic, Mr. Hassan. Is that true?" Mr. Hassan nodded an agreeable "yes." I explained our report card predicament and asked if he would help us. He agreed and took the English version of the card from my hand. Two days later he called to say the card was ready. The paper was in his hand as he smiled his usual ready smile when I walked into his office.

Mr. Hassan was different from most of those who lived and worked in the First Ward, a small section of Lackawanna where each building had acquired an orange hue from the iron oxide that poured daily from the stacks of the steel plant. The smell of chemicals, iron, and hydrogen sulfide permeated the air and a high percentage of the residents suffered from a wide range of respiratory ailments. I knew nothing of his background except that he traveled each day to Friendship House from Buffalo, a scant two miles away.

I like to think my liberal views protect me from prejudice, but I realize my view of Mr. Hassan was clouded by the cataracts of middle-class suburban living. I was skeptical that an accountant could handle the language required to translate a report card. Worse, I figured Mr. Hassan was working in the First Ward because he probably couldn't get a job anywhere else.

As Mr. Hassan handed the card to me he said, "You'll have to be careful here, Mr. Graves. Arabic goes in just the opposite direction from the English. You have to have your columns go from right to left instead of from left to right."

I looked down at the three-page report card, noting the aesthetics of the swoops, lines, dots, and half moons that made up the Arabic writing. Mr. Hassan had done the job but I had no way of checking the accuracy of his translations. I thanked him and left wondering if I had done the right thing.

"Well, here it is Mary," I said as I passed her the pages. I felt as though I was passing on some strange currency I didn't understand. "What do you think?"

"My God, Don, I hope this says what we hope it says." We went to work on the eight to ten report cards, carefully double-checking each other to make sure we had checked the columns in reverse order. We chatted as we worked side by side.

"Suppose they compare these and we've made a mistake? Will some father feel that we have disgraced his son? Will there be arguments between husband and wife? Suppose Mr. Hassan has insulted them with his interpretation of what we are trying to do?" We were both well versed in the dangers of Semitic insult. Two weeks before an Arab child pulled a knife on a Spanish-speaking classmate. The Spanish speaker laughed at something the Arab child was eating and the knife appeared instantaneously. An implied insult brought immediate results.

We sent the report card home that afternoon. Mary and I decided to keep each other company in the basement of the church to be available in case misunderstandings occurred. Occasionally we glanced at the clock, mentally tracking the time the report cards would arrive at the children's homes. The children were dismissed at three. At three-thirty we heard a loud banging on the outside door. I looked at Mary. She looked at me and moved closer to my chair.

I made the long trip up the stairs and opened the church door. Mohammed Mohammed, one of the older brothers of the children, stood in the doorway with a large crowd of adults. His eyes were blazing. "Who has written this?" he shouted, waving the report card papers in the air. The crowd murmured.

"I did," I gulped, hoping Mr. Hassan's work day at Friendship House was over and he had escaped to Buffalo.

"You know Arabic?" he gestured in surprise, moving closer to me.

"Well, no."

"Then who has written this?"

"Uh, Mr. Hassan . . . over at Friendship House." I prayed that he would not be assaulted for his helpfulness.

Mohammed turned to the delegation and waved his arms amidst a torrent of Arabic. He turned back to me. "Mr. Graves," his voice had quieted now. "Come, we must meet this man, for he is a poet!"

Much later I learned that Mr. Hassan had written what could almost be called a religious document speaking of Allah's grace and caring for each child, and that he had enriched each category on the card beyond our terse language about skills. Perhaps we should have poets write our report cards.

Fear contributes to prejudice. I feared for my own safety because of some prior incidents in the First Ward of Lackawanna. Usually we'd find a reliable native speaker who could mediate misunderstandings. In the case of the Arabs I wasn't sure whom to ask. Under normal circumstances the Arabian families were hospitable, caring, and eager for their children to acquire an education. But now we were in the position of judging the worth of their children's efforts. I told myself that Mr. Hassan, a mere accountant, wouldn't know how to translate the report card correctly.

I've since learned that poets are everywhere, although unfortunately, most recognize that the world does not readily accept them. Speak about your own poetry, however, and fellow poets come out of the woodwork.

Sometimes I wonder if report cards for different ethnic groups might not benefit from a reporting system that matched the culture.

TRY THIS: Think back to a time when your own prejudices surprised you and subsequent events showed your initial impressions were unfounded. Or think back to when fear brought out protective judgments that were prejudicial. Tell the story.

Exer-Genie

The exercise fad began in the early to mid-1960s. Since I was beginning to be terrified about the onset of middle age, I was receptive to the latest approaches to exercise, strength training, anything that promised to maintain a youthful appearance.

Isometric exercise entered the national scene at about that time. Isometrics could be done at home, at work, or while sitting at your desk. They promised strength. The best isometrics provide continued resistance. I could, for example, sit at my desk at the church and press against the desktop for a count of thirty. But that didn't cost money. If I was serious about exercise I ought to spend some money.

When I heard about the Exer-Genie, of its use by the Buffalo Bills, then the leaders of the American Football League, various high school coaches, and some of my friends, I decided that it was time to show I was serious about exercise.

The Exer-Genie is made up of a nylon rope that passes around and through a stainless steel spindle. Turn the dial on the spindle and the tension on the nylon rope is increased. One end of the rope is hooked to a board on the floor, the other end, with the spindle in between, has a handle to pull. The Exer-Genie, unlike weight lifting, offers constant resistance. I set my dial for one hundred pounds, hook the rope into the eye on the floorboard, and pull on the handle until it is over my head. Thus I have one hundred pounds of constant pull. But if I lift one hundred pounds of weights I have a different problem. Once the weights are in motion, their actual weight, because of inertia, is not one hundred pounds but something much lighter.

Each morning I challenged my manhood with the Exer-Genie in my upstairs bedroom. I gradually increased the number of repetitions and the amount of resistance to 125 pounds. I could also check my profile in the mirror, imagining that my muscles were growing and my middle becoming flatter.

The entire household could hear Dad snorting and puffing on his machine. I growled and gasped until I finally brought the handle up and over my head. My daughter Caroline, seven years old and a wiry forty-six pounds, watched me huff, cocked her head, and said, "Let me try it, Dad."

"No, you'll kill yourself. Leave it alone."

"Just once, Dad. I won't get hurt." Caroline had one of those high-pitched voices, persistent like a mosquito when it smells blood.

Each morning I'd practice and Caroline usually came in to observe, then beg for a chance to try it. She usually did her begging when I was straining most to go the final eighteen inches over my head. I'd reach the apex and sometimes yell at her, "I can't talk now, Caroline. I don't want to argue. Leave me alone." Caroline would pout, turn on her heel, and stomp back to her room.

One morning after working out, showering, and shaving I heard the rattle of the hook going through the eyebolt on the Exer-Genie board. I hurried my dressing and just as I turned the corner from bathroom to bedroom, I saw Caroline pushing the handle of the Exer-Genie, with the one hundred pound test just as I'd left it, the final six inches over her head. Her face was red, her jaw set, and with torso, legs, and arms driving, she drove the handle the final distance.

When she reached the peak, her face broke into a triumphant smile. She clumped the equipment to the floor and with blazing blue eyes announced, "Told you I could do it!" and stomped out of the room.

As I recall I only used the Exer-Genie for another month after Caroline's demonstration. Reflecting on this incident some three decades later I realize that the Exer-Genie event was a metaphor for much of what was to come in her life. She was always in a hurry to keep up with and outperform her two older sisters. She graduated early from high school, at nineteen was first to be married, and had the first grandchild but didn't decide to go to college until she was twenty-eight.

This year she is Chief Resident in Obstetrics and Gynecology at Maine Medical Center in Portland, Maine. I hear her words, "Told you I could do it."

I've found that I continually underestimate the drive of some people to learn, especially in my own family. Caroline was our number three daughter who wanted to do everything her older sisters could do. In some cases, like the Exer-Genie, she wanted to show her father he wasn't so far ahead either.

To some degree Caroline knew her own strength better than I did. She could go hand over hand up a rope without using her feet. When our son and an older boy couldn't get a cement lawn roller out of a ditch, they asked Caroline to help. She grabbed the handle and with a twist of her body and the application of sudden force, the roller jumped out. She knew what she could do.

Our children and our students often know what they can do better than we do. The best learning situations allow for mutual challenge, teacher to student, student to teacher.

TRY THIS: Recall a challenging moment when you underestimated what your children or your students could do. Write or tell that story.

Independence

In Toronto, three video cameras rolled under an elaborate array of kleig lights. The floor was a tangle of power lines and camera cables. Between the cameras and the cables sixty teachers focused on Mary Ellen Giacobbe as she demonstrated teaching writing with eight five- to seven-year-old children.

The children worked on the floor with eighteen-by-twenty-four-inch sheets of plain or lined newsprint. The teachers and cameras picked up details of children's drawing and writing on the large sheets and listened to Mary Ellen as she quietly spoke with the children. Some children drew, others wrote, and a few stopped to get more paper to add on to work they had already completed.

One child went to the side of the work area to staple a new section to the bottom of his paper. The stapler jammed. The child pushed the stapler to connect the two pieces. Again, the stapler failed to function. The child left the work area and approached Mary Ellen. "Teacher, I can't make this work."

I thought Mary Ellen might say, "Well, then take another stapler." Even though the cameras were rolling and the lights burning, and sixty sets of eyes watched, Mary Ellen dealt with the problem as she would in her own classroom. She lowered herself to the child's eyes level, looked into his eyes, and asked, "If it doesn't work, what can you do?" For a moment the child looked puzzled, not used to teachers turning the problem back to him. He thought for a moment, unaware of the full silence of a room full of teachers, then spoke.

"I guess I could write it, cut it off and then put it on with paper clips." The child didn't stay centered on fixing a stapler.

He came up with an approach that bypassed the need for a stapler. Best of all, in solving this problem Mary Ellen established a principle that allowed him to bypass her in the future.

I should have known that Mary Ellen wouldn't change her approach to teaching young children to write, even in the middle of a video recording that would be played for many other teachers. Mary Ellen emphasizes children's independence, no matter where it applied. It just happened that she was teaching writing. Working with a jammed stapler was an essential part of the writing process.

In 1978 I began to observe Mary Ellen's classroom as part of a two-year in-depth study of how children learned to write. The study, funded by the National Institute of Education, was conducted in Atkinson, New Hampshire. Mary Ellen's classroom was one of nine in which we observed children learning to write. Each year she has increased children's responsibilities as she has learned more about what they can do.

As Mary Ellen was learning how to give children more independence, I gathered data and learned from her about writing and about child responsibility. She knew how to wait. Two years after the lights and the cameras in Toronto she was in a television studio in Harrisburg, Pennsylvania. A still larger group of teachers were present to observe her demonstrate with eight fearful third-grade children. As they entered the room their eyes grew large, taking in the lights, cameras, and teachers circling the room. The video cameras were even more imposing than in Toronto. We had asked for eight very different children. We got them: two African American, two Spanish-speaking, one Asian, and three white children; four boys and four girls. (Later, we found out that the children had no experience with writing and had been sitting for an hour in another room in the studio with their hands folded.)

Mary Ellen began in her usual enthusiastic manner. She leaned forward in her chair, engaged the children's eyes, and said in a musical-sounding voice, "We're going to be doing some interesting things today. I'm interested in some of the things you've been reading. Some authors in your books. Do you have some favorite authors?"

No answer. Mary Ellen waited, allowing a long pause before she spoke again. "I know you've got lots of authors running through your heads that you'd like to share."

Another long silence. Finally, one boy said, "Dr. Seuss."

"Oh, Dr. Seuss, and what has he written that you like?"

"*Green Eggs and Ham.*"

"Could you tell me more about that?" But the child wasn't able to say any more. "Anyone else have some authors or books?"

More silence. The children didn't seem restless, but the audience of teachers began to rustle in their seats, struggling on behalf of the children and Mary Ellen. I wondered if anything would happen that would help the teachers and the children learn.

Mary Ellen suddenly shifted her approach. "I'm sure you know stories of your own. Tell me about some things that have happened to you." More silence. Finally, the same boy who had mentioned Dr. Seuss began to tell about a football game he just played. Mary Ellen drew about five sentences from him while the other children observed the lone volunteer.

A boy to the left and middle raised his hand. His eyes and face were expressionless. He spoke in a monotone, "I love my father."

"You love your father, Ralph?" replied Mary Ellen, reading the name pinned on his shirt. She reflected his own language back to him but asked him to tell her more.

"Yeah, he was driving upstate when these crazy kids in a buggy ran into the side of 'em. He got all smashed up. He's in the hospital but he doesn't know anybody."

Once Ralph spoke, Mary Ellen was greeted with a barrage of hands. The Vietnamese girl told how she couldn't tell the bus driver in English how to find her home on the first day of school; another told about her pet. Soon the children were listing topics to write about while Mary Ellen moved around the studio listening. Later, they shared their pieces with each other. Ralph shared his written story about his father.

After sixty-nine intense minutes, Mary Ellen said, "Well, boys and girls, you've worked very hard this morning. I've learned about soccer, football, a father, baseball, and getting lost. Thank you for coming." She began to organize her papers to leave, but Ralph's hand was up.

"One more thing," Ralph said as he jabbed a finger at the bottom of his page, "one more thing." He then read haltingly, but with an expectant tone, "My father's . . . going . . . to be all right."

No matter how many people are watching or how pressured the event, Mary Ellen Giacobbe does not change her approach to teaching. She knows that her ultimate objective is a respectful independence on the part of the child. Every opportunity for teaching contributes across the board to other children's learning. She establishes very basic principles. Above all, she focuses on children as problem solvers. She refrains from the extensive use of praise and allows the child to say to herself, "I have done that successfully." Praise is often manipulative. It establishes us as someone who authenticates another person's learning. Good teachers help children know for themselves that they are the authors of real learning.

TRY THIS: Think of a learning situation in which the learner no longer needs you or better still, in which the learner can congratulate herself for learning. Tell or write the story.

Learning Speeds

I've learned from my own children. Even though I pride myself on preparing students to be good teachers, I'm constantly jolted by my children's ability to raise tough questions about my teaching at home. Indeed, if my university students could speak with the abandon of an adolescent son or daughter, I'd learn much more about teaching than I know at the moment.

Back in the mid-1980s my daughter Laura was learning how to drive. I pride myself on patience but my feet often belie my underlying restlessness. When Laura drives I press down on an imaginary brake. I press on the accelerator to get the car moving. If Laura doesn't respond quickly enough I calmly make comments: "Slow down." "You can go now." "Very good, now watch out for that car up there that is going to turn from his driveway."

One warm October day, when I was in a great hurry to get to the university and back again, Laura occupied the driver's seat. She'd been driving only three weeks and needed to practice for her driver education class. She stalled several times backing out of our winding driveway. Then she stalled four more times getting back over the high crown of the street at the end of the driveway.

Two tenths of a mile down our short road, at a rural highway, Laura paused to examine traffic. She waited at least twenty seconds, checking left and right according to the best driver's manual. I itched. On her second check she spotted a car a quarter of a mile away. She waited for the car to pass. I writhed. About the time the first car drew abreast of our own, she spotted another car at least a half mile down the road. We didn't move.

"Laura, for heaven's sake, you can go now," I moaned. "Come on, let's get to town."

"Dad," Laura answered with unusual politeness, "you're telling me to go when *you* would go. I can't go when *you* would, because I'm me. I'm slow at this and if I'm not going to get ploughed, you'd better let me do it at my speed."

I think Laura was so patient with me because she was so right. How easy it is to command someone to go at your own speed. I'd been driving for thirty-five years and Laura for three weeks. Why should she enter a road at my speed?

I used the example the following Tuesday in my course on teaching writing. One of the teachers was asking a child to do something, but the child neither understood, nor could he match his learning speed to the complexity of the teacher's instruction. It takes time and good observation to match teaching and learning speeds.

I've drawn on this story countless times, which doesn't mean I tell it to others as much as I implicitly apply it to myself in teaching/learning situations.

Teaching within the family is quite an event. Betty and I have raised five kids, four of whom are parents themselves. It is always interesting to see them teach their children as we tried to teach them. Their second drafts are better than our first. Teaching goes on from generation to generation.

If we do the job well, we teach children how to help us teach them. Of course, their responses can often be quite abrupt, as in Laura's case. "You're telling me to go when *you* would go." You're you and I'm me. The art of teaching is to adjust for individual learning speeds yet have very high expectations.

Around the time I was helping her learn to drive, I observed Laura teaching her four-year-old niece, Margaret, how to set the table. "The knife and spoon are very good friends, Margaret. They like to talk face to face over on this side away from the prickly fork. Put your finger on the end of this fork and feel how prickly Mr. Fork is." Laura then passed the knife, fork, and spoon to Margaret to see if she could carry out the demonstration. Margaret did it correctly except that she had the handle of the spoon upright and reversed. Laura laughed and said, "Oh, you're so funny Margaret, you've got the spoon's feet talking to the knife's face. Now put them so they can really talk." Laura's teaching followed Margaret's attempt to set the table with humor and patience. Today Laura is a special education teacher in the state of Maine.

TRY THIS: Think of a situation in which you noticed that your teaching speed outstripped the other person's learning speed. Write or tell this story and share it. Or consider a time when a student's learning speed was faster than your teaching speed.

The Voice Coach

I had to deliver a manuscript to the Ford Foundation in four weeks. Their guideline was a simple one: "Write a monograph about the status of writing in the United States." But I couldn't write. My desk and study were covered with piles of data, folders of facts, notebooks filled with interviews, and photocopied articles on the status of writing.

I wrote each morning but the language was dead, the ideas listless. I kept rewriting but the fourth rewrite read worse than the first draft. Here I was, trying to write a piece persuading Americans that there was a crisis in writing and I was part of the crisis. I was a fraud. I called Don Murray.

"I can't write, Don. I've got this whole pile of junk and I'm going nowhere. I think I know what I want to say. I've got good data but the harder I try to write, the worse it gets."

"Come on down and I'll give it a look." Murray's deep bass voice conveyed the assurance of a brain surgeon contemplating minor surgery. Murray had reason to be confident. He'd received a Pulitzer Prize in editorial writing, served as an editor at *Time* magazine, written several novels, and published more than 250 articles as a freelance writer. That didn't count the dozens of books he'd written about how to write.

Murray's house was only three miles away. It was long enough on that hot August day in 1976 for me to rehearse what might happen. We'd been speaking daily about writing for the previous three years. He'd mentored me through my first three years as an assistant professor at the University of New Hampshire. He would take my pages, flip his glasses to his forehead, and read with the speed of light while sliding his hand down the right side of the page. His diagnosis would be instantaneous, usually pointing out one redeemable sentence or paragraph on which to build a better piece.

That day I was desperate. Murray would have to be at his psychological best to help me through the brick wall of writer's block. I hoped there was an outside chance that the writing might be better than I thought. After all, two weeks of work on four pages might possibly be a solid opening to the project.

I turned the corner onto Faculty Road, motoring down through lovely suburban homes in our small college town. I turned right on to Mill Pond Road. Three houses left to back out. "Shit," I said to myself, "What have I got to lose?" and whipped left into the steep-sloped driveway.

I didn't have to ring. Murray was looking for me as he usually does when I call ahead. He filled the door: a large head, white hair, blue eyes, a white beard, an open, short-sleeved shirt, an imposing stomach, khaki trousers. "Come on in." His voice wasn't cheery, just medical, like the doctor's when he swings the door open for your annual physical.

I'd been at Murray's home at least twenty-five times in the three years since we met. Today, more than ever, as I entered the house from the garage I was aware of Don's books. Don's life is books and writing, writing and books. Books were stuffed from floor to ceiling on all sides of this twelve-by-eighteen-foot room, occasionally punctuated by a window or a door. "He's literate, so damned literate." I knew that his real library was in his study. This was old stuff, read long ago, but retired for easier access.

We turned left and entered his living room, the large, curved couch piled high with newspapers: the local paper, *Foster's Daily Democrat*, a pile for the *New York Times*, another for the *Boston Globe*. He sprinted through the papers each day, reading them for himself and all his friends. I received at least three or four clippings a week from him then and twenty-one years later I still do. Dozens of people receive letters with clippings just as I do.

"Sit down. Want some iced tea?"

"Thanks, no. Let's get this over with. It hurts too damned much," I said as I passed him the four pages, my total output for two weeks of work.

He flipped the glasses to his forehead. I'd studied Murray

many times before while he read my papers. The blue eyes were intent, betraying no emotion, just clinical interest. I wondered if there was an outside chance the pages were good.

Two minutes later, he was done. He said nothing but stared at the ceiling. Murray's diagnosis was usually swift and unrelenting in its honesty. If it was junk he'd say so if he thought I could take it.

He sighed, pursed his lips, and said, "I'd like to try something on you I've never had the guts to try on myself. You game?"

He'd given no diagnosis, but he'd offered a solution, something gutsy perhaps, or bizarre. At least the novelty might make my work more interesting.

"Sure. Go ahead. What have you got in mind?"

"Be back in a minute." Murray returned with an empty box that once held a ream of paper in one hand. In the other he carried a long kitchen knife. He took the knife and ceremoniously began to cut a long, thin hole across the box lid. He didn't appear to be used to tasks that demanded this kind of dexterity.

"What the hell is all this about?" I asked. I couldn't stand the unusual silence.

"You'll see." Murray's solutions to my writing problems were usually much more straightforward. He'd say something like "Doesn't sound like you. Just say it."

After Murray had completed cutting a nine-and-a-half-inch-wide slot across the top of the box he reached for masking tape and sealed all the edges. "There," he announced. "It's done. Now here's what I want you to do."

"I want you to write starting tomorrow morning, but when you write you can't change anything. When you get to the bottom of the page, take the sheet out of your typewriter and stick it through the slot into the box. You can't look back."

"Geez, Don, what about the references?"

"Forget the references. You know your subject. What you forget, the reader shouldn't have to suffer through. Just write. Tomorrow night you bring the box down here; I'll read the stuff and tell you if it's any good."

I stared at the box. I looked at Murray, who rose from his chair. When Murray's lumbering frame rises, that's the signal to leave. Usually, he leads up to it by shifting his feet. I'd missed the cue.

The next day I cleared the tables and put references and piles of data and early drafts back into their folders. Finally, when the table and typewriter stand were clear of everything, I vacuumed my study.

I began to type. I started talking through my fingers, not worrying about language, just telling the story about our national problems in writing. At the end of half an hour I'd written two pages, and by the end of the day I'd written about ten thousand words.

That night I took the box down to Murray, confident that the writing, and the output, was good. "Now this sounds like you. It's twice, no, four times better than what you wrote before. You know your subject; just keep writing."

By the end of the week I'd written about 110 pages of fairly good stuff. Thanks to Murray I'd found my voice. Even though I cut the final report to twenty-eight pages, I never lost my voice again after he gave me the magic box.

Don Murray is the consummate writing teacher. He knows writing from two sides, that of the teacher and that of the writer. I would add a third, the voice of the writer. He quickly finds out what a writer knows, brings it out in conversation, and then locates the writer's voice in the text. I've built a career on what he taught me with the sealed box. Rapid writing is something I rely on in my teaching. My students do innumerable ten-minute writing stints with no editing. If I have six writing tasks ahead of me and I find my mind jamming up, I give each a rapid five to ten minutes of writing just to get them moving and feel a sense of peace. Rapid writing lets the uncensored voice in. Of course, the art of writing is in the rewriting. And rewriting is based on a no-nonsense ability to recognize your own authentic voice in the text.

We've all had teachers like Murray who spot our authentic self in the artwork, the song, the essay, or the dance. They know their craft so well, they can spot what is authentic.

TRY THIS: Recall a teacher who spotted your voice, something authentic about you, and tell the story surrounding the event when that happened. Take ten minutes and write rapidly without changing anything.

You Jerk!

Late one Friday afternoon in February I sat at my desk at the University of New Hampshire. I watched a light flurry of snow float gently to the ground. There weren't any students walking through the corridors. I began to think of the writing I needed to complete on the weekend, at the same time wishing I could find a way to get in some cross-country skiing.

Buzz on the intercom. "Call for you, Don. Take it on 79."

The voice on the other end spoke rapidly. "I'm xxxx from xxxx, could we have a short interview on some of your views about writing?" I remembered the last part, "Could we have an interview about writing?" In those days in 1977 I was ready to talk with anyone who wanted to know what I thought about writing. I was hungry for a chance to get my views before the public.

"Sure, fire away."

"Why do you think writing is important, Professor Graves?"

"Well, first of all, in a democracy it is important for the governed to have the will and ability to respond to the government. Writing is a tool for thinking. It is a way of finding out what you think."

The man went on. Within fifteen minutes the interview was completed. I thanked him and hung up the phone. As the phone touched the receiver it occurred to me that I had forgotten to ask who he was or what publication he represented. I frequently forget names when I am first introduced or when I only catch a name over the telephone.

I expected I'd hear from the interviewer when the article was published. Weeks went by. I heard nothing. By the middle of April I decided I must have been one of a series of people interviewed for the same article and had simply been dropped. Still, I felt good about the interview and wondered who the interviewer might have been.

During the second week of June I went up to the departmental office to retrieve the daily mail from my cubby. My box was filled with letters, and a box on the floor with still more, all addressed to me.

I pulled the first letter off the top, checked the postmark, and read "Rochester." I figured it was a letter from Rochester, New Hampshire. I broke the seal and read the first line: "You Jerk! You are playing into the hands of the Communists with subversive thinking." Inside was a diagram of sharks eating smaller fish, which ate still smaller fish. A hammer and sickle was marked on the side of the large shark. I had no idea what the letter was about.

I opened the second letter. It was equally vitriolic but at least the respondent had enclosed a small clipping reporting my interview with a correspondent from the *National Enquirer*. A gentleman wrote, "You say we live in a democracy and I say, 'What democracy!'" I read the clipping prepared to jump on gross inaccuracies. I couldn't. The article was completely accurate. In fact, it was more accurate about my views than a piece published three years later in *Time* magazine.

I read all the mail carefully and learned that the *Enquirer* is read by the extreme political left and the extreme right, and by shut-ins. I answered all the mail from the shut-ins because they probably figured that a writer would most likely respond to their letters. That one two-hundred-word article produced more letters than all the articles in *Time* magazine, *Psychology Today*, the *Christian Science Monitor*, and a syndicated piece put out by the Associated Press combined.

It's a good thing I didn't know that the interviewer was from the *National Enquirer*. My answers would have been guarded, my text convoluted, and the resulting article a confused jumble. I didn't have a chance to apply my prejudice.

I was naturally astounded by the initiative demonstrated by the extreme right and left of the political spectrum. They have no problem picking up a pen and going to work. Their monological voices spring into action at a moment's notice. On the other hand, the political center is very quiet. Listen to the talk shows; the far left and right are ably represented.

TRY THIS: Think of a situation in which you have been misunderstood by another person, group, or the press. Write about the misunderstanding. How did it affect you?

Choices

Three of us sat over dinner at the Pump House in Fairbanks, Alaska, in June 1983. The fourth, Paul Ondooguk, ordered only dessert but talked for three hours. From him we learned about tough choices.

Ondooguk was teaching for the summer at the University of Alaska at Fairbanks. He was there to teach young Inupiats like himself to prepare for big choices in 1994, when the U.S. Congress had determined that Inupiats could exercise their choice to sell their land or keep it for themselves and the tribe. The land sits on an ocean of oil, and Inupiats know that oil companies can bring near insuperable pressure on villages and weak individuals to sell.

Each summer the brightest Inupiat high school juniors are brought to the university to study the 1994 law, their culture, and political action and organization. The nation plans to continue the study program until 1994, when an educated group would be prepared to deal with the anticipated pressures.

Ondooguk's ice cream melted as he spoke, his great prow of a head leaning forward. Dark shiny eyes over high cheekbones and a jut-jaw beard with premature streaks of white framed his measured words. Paul Ondooguk already had a master's degree in education from the University of Washington. He wondered, "Should I get a doctorate, be an educator, or become a great hunter? Should the Inupiats preserve their culture or be educated and take their place in the twenty-first century?"

"I am growing old, you see. As a hunter I only have a high school education. My father and uncles have doctoral degrees in hunting. The time is getting late for me to be a hunter. Let me show you what I mean.

"I have seen my father walk through a valley for the first time on a hunting trip and look over the trees, boulders, and scrub. When he returns to that same valley five years later on another hunting trip, he knows all those rocks and trees. He already has a map in his head and he walks as if he is walking in his own home looking for game.

"I have seen uncles in the fog at sea, with the ice floes and the wind blowing, look at the color of the water and know where they are.

"We kill to live. We hunt to live. When you hunt you are at the edge of living. When I went to the University of Washington I used to walk up into the mountains and through the trees and valleys. But there were no animals there to teach you respect, respect for the life you held that you might lose. You lose something in living if there is no edge to it . . . no danger.

"People think we kill for nothing, that we hate animals. We love animals. We respect them and they respect us. How can we hate animals when we know them as our brothers, all the habits, the way they must kill to eat, the way they raise their young? We tell stories about these great animals, stories that are filled with respect about their intelligence and great spirit.

"Take the great whale, the bowhead, and how they tell us we cannot hunt them." Ondooguk leaned back in his chair and shook his head. He sighed, opened his palms, sighed, leaned back again and forward, then hissed, "It makes me so angry I cannot speak.

"We kill twenty-eight bowheads a year to feed our people. Feed them. And we use everything, bones, skin, entrails, baleen. We waste nothing. The International Whaling Commission comes to do their census. They, who have slaughtered whales for profit, who use up the resources of the deep, now come to tell us we can't kill twenty-eight whales, when there are plenty.

"Do you know how they do their whale census? They stop at the first ice floe and count.

"You cannot count from there, we say. Come out on to the ice to the open water where you can see.

"Oh, that is too dangerous, they say. And they come up three thousand whales short of our census while standing on the first floes.

"And we are not slaughtering whales with weapons of war mounted on our prows, but the old way, with umiaks. It takes courage and skill even to approach a whale, much less kill one, strip it, and eat it.

"And so it goes, the old way and the new ways to do things. I have gotten a good grant at our school in Kotzebue to make videotapes of our old hunters and craftspersons in our village. I wanted to make good videos of them before they died out. I brought in this TV man who was used to producing big stuff. I think he was Australian. He kept saying, 'Where's the talent?'

"I laughed, 'Where's the talent?' But I knew what he meant.

"I'd take him to my uncle who builds kayaks. We got videos of my uncle from the time he went out to choose the right trees, to the right wood in the trees, the skins, and all the rest. We got the details, then we had the young men try to make a kayak from the video like he did. They tried and worked very hard and finally finished one. We called in the old man, who walked all around the kayak, studying it. Then he said, 'It's a bummer, but it'll float. It is good enough.' We don't want our young men to lose all these traditions and skills. They will soon disappear if we don't do something about it.

"And so we have videos of men hunting the seal, walrus, building umiaks step by step. Of course, the video is not enough, but it will show what these old people can do, what we have to lose."

My wife, Betty, made the mistake of asking Paul about the killing of pup seals. "Ha, pup seals, Greenpeace," he snorted. "Greenpeace doesn't care about conservation; all they care about is making money. The pup seal isn't endangered; he just has cute, big eyes. Now there's a walrus off the coast of Hawaii that is truly endangered, but he has the misfortune to be ugly. Do you think Greenpeace is interested in protecting him? Heck no! All these people in the lower forty-eight trying to mix moneymaking and conservation with a land, animals, and people they don't know."

Paul was used to making tough decisions. His father was Inupiat, his mother a Caucasian nurse, who died when he was very young. His father numbed himself with alcohol, and Paul and his four brothers more or less raised themselves. As a young man in his late teens Paul became heavily involved with alcohol and small-time crime. He turned himself around with tough decisions not to drink and to get an education. He looked sideways, saw the broken lives of his friends, and decided he would take a different course.

He decided what he would affirm, then what he wouldn't do. "Today I think I will be a hunter. It is the selfish thing to do. I will do what I am trying to preserve in my culture. Education can wait. I can always study later on."

Paul forced me to reexamine my own values about whales, wildlife, and an alternative way of living. My wife and I still carry some of his language with us: "There is nothing there to teach you respect" or, "It's a bummer, but it'll float." I find that people from another culture provide new language that forces us to reexamine our own values and culture.

The lynx no longer lives in our area of northern New Hampshire. Large highways cut our local lynx off from other strains of the species in Canada. When the genetic pool was significantly depleted, the species died out. Without fresh ideas from people like Paul Ondooguk to challenge us, our thinking will not be regenerated. We must carry stories of other cultures as they have affected us firsthand that we may appreciate the gifts of their ideas.

TRY THIS: Review your contacts with other cultures as an adult. Think of a time when you encountered that culture in your neighborhood or community, in travel or at work. Tell the story of that meeting. Discuss what you took from that culture and still use.

The Bus Driver

Betty and I wanted to buy some sheepskin rugs before we ended our Australian visit. The night before I had addressed the Primary English Teacher's Association's tenth anniversary banquet, and only one day remained to complete our shopping. We consulted the man in the Bondi Hotel lobby about transport and where to get good sheepskin. He recommended taking the bus to Bondi Junction.

We were staying at Bondi Beach and Bondi Junction was only a fifteen-minute ride away. I was used to traveling on buses in the United Kingdom, where the drivers didn't seem too pleased to have passengers. American bus drivers weren't far behind. I wasn't prepared for my first Australian driver.

"Good morning, sir." Halfway up the stairs onto the bus I glanced up to see the author of the voice. A young man in cap and uniform was smiling at me, not the usual bureaucratic smile but one that seemed to enjoy my entrance.

"And good morning, madam, lovely jacket you're wearing today," he addressed Betty, behind me.

I fumbled for change. "How much, sir?" I began to echo his language and style.

"Only thirty, sir. No hurry."

I found the change and honestly felt no need to hurry. I looked around at the other passengers. Their faces didn't bear the usual strained get-the-shopping-out-of-the-way looks. I soon found out why.

As our bus left the beach area and the streets got busier, the corners were filled with waiting passengers who pressed their way onto the bus. Our driver never changed his style. He had something different, something unique to say to each person at about the time they were halfway up the stairs.

"Good morning, miss. Nice day to go to town."

"Lovely suit, sets you right up for a good day in town."

"Step right up. Step right up. We're all here together. Kindly move to the rear please."

"Can I help you ma'am? Got much to carry, haven't you." With that remark the driver sprang from his seat and helped an elderly woman up the last high step into the bus. He did the same for a young woman carrying a child in her arms.

Betty and I were seated halfway back. We looked across the aisle at the other passengers, who were smiling and nudging each other with a few "have you seen a character like this before?" shakes of their heads.

"Quite a person, isn't he?" I asked, more as a comment to the passenger next to me. "Do you know him? Does he always handle this run?" I couldn't decide if people were caught up, like me, in the driver's spirit or if they already knew him.

"Never seen 'im before. Must be new. Some character. They'll knock that out of 'im soon enough." By now at least fifteen or so of the passengers were looking forward to his words between stops, more I think to see the effect of the driver's strategy on the new passengers. I began to hope the trip to Bondi Junction would last more than the scheduled twenty minutes.

Six passengers queued at the next corner stop. "Good morning all," burst the driver, in time to meet the opening bus doors. "Lovely day." Heads snapped up in unexpected wonder. The driver caught them in mid-bewilderment with another salvo. "Thank you for traveling with us. Kindly step carefully. Watch yourselves. The last step is a big one."

"Hi laddy, grab the railing. My, what a strong pull!" The driver especially enjoyed children and the elderly. His verbal patter, almost as rapid as a radio announcer at a basketball game, quickly diagnosed each passenger's individuality, the one remark needed to make that person a member of the bus club. I began to wonder if he planned his statements as he spotted new passengers a block away.

I began to think ahead for him, as did the other passengers. I looked for mothers and children, older persons, as if we were all conducting a "brighten the day" clinic for everyone boarding the bus. Occasionally, we turned to look at our newfound bus friends. Within the space of two miles we had become a group of people who knew each other in a cursory yet familial way. We were a temporary family with a freedom we hadn't known when we got on the bus.

We arrived all too soon at Bondi Junction. Each of us made it a point to thank the driver as we departed. "Nice day. Thank you for the ride."

Some asked questions, "Are you married? Have kids?" He wasn't married. A few said nothing, but all made it a point to give him an appreciative look. I said I was from America and thanked him for showing me what one person could do to help people be glad to know each other.

About once a week I bring up the story of the bus driver. He had genius, first to observe the person, then capture them in a line, helping total strangers become members of a community.

As one of the passengers observed, "They'll knock that out of 'im soon enough," but I don't think so. The driver was having too good a time carrying out his mission. As we left the bus we all put in our own versions of the one-line blessing.

I've seen good teachers do the equivalent of the bus driver on the first day of school. They have a way of building an instant community by making unique observations about individual children. Our lives can be so fast paced, we too easily lose the freshness of the caring one-line comment.

TRY THIS: Take one day to experiment with the fresh one-line observation. At the end of the day, stop and quickly write one or two stories that unfolded from your observations.

Twin Learning

Sometimes it is useful to try to learn something you know very little about. Indeed, it might be something you may never do again because the process is so foreign to your nature. I say this because it is always useful to observe yourself dealing with the rudiments of learning. You stand back and ask yourself, "Is this the way I would best learn this?" Your instructor may have an entirely different style of learning. Somewhere in the midst of this tutelage, you and the instructor must work it out between you.

I also recommend reversing the process and having your last teacher become your student. You will now teach your teacher how to learn something he or she knows little about. Again, you will negotiate your way, constructing the best teaching/learning situation you can.

My wife, Betty, tried to teach me how to operate a sewing machine. I, in turn, tried to teach Betty how to watch a basketball game.

THE SEWING MACHINE

I've been only a distant observer of the sewing scene. My mother sewed, first using a treadle machine, then in the forties an electric Singer. Betty sewed even more than Mother, making dress after dress for our four daughters. From time to time she'd call from the next room, "Come look at this dress. What do you think?" I'd look and nod approvingly, but ignore the machinery of the process she was following. The males in my generation of the Graves family have a genetic predisposition for ignoring the mechanical. We believe, as my father taught us, that touching machines and things electrical only makes matters worse.

My memories of thread and yarn are even more unhappy. In first grade, because of the John Dewey influence in the early thirties, I had to make an overcast stitch (my wife later told me it was an overcast stitch; I didn't remember the term) along the border edge of a piece of cloth, but I simply couldn't hold the needle so that the tip would perforate the cloth, or if it did, I couldn't get it to come back through. Making stitches an even distance from the edge along a whole side was well beyond my reach. Overcasting for me was a fiasco.

At the height of World War II, every student in our eighth grade, male or female, knitted squares, which were then sewed together into blankets for delivery to Great Britain. All good citizens, young and old, had to do their part. I couldn't and have suffered mild guilt when saluting the American flag ever since. I'd knit ten stitches, drop two, regain my digital composure, and knit a few more. Three dismal, bunched up rows were my total production at the end of the week. Then Alice Winderknecht took pity on me and finished my square in fifteen minutes. (I will remind her of her kindness at our fiftieth reunion in 1998.)

Thus, learning to use a sewing machine was not a venture into the promised land. Still, in the spirit of pure experimentation, I learned. Here is what I wrote when I finished.

"This is a spool," Betty said, pointing to a spool of blue thread on top of the machine. "The thread starts here. Now, if you want to know how the thread gets on here I can show you that."

"Better wait," I said. I could see that a long chain of moves lay ahead with the threading of the machine.

"Now take the thread and first move it through the hook, then down here, around this reel, snap it back so it catches, and then up here . . ."

"Whoa, that's far enough," I said. "I'll never remember this. I think I could handle about four of those steps and that's all. I've got to try it, okay?" She let me thread the first five steps. My ability to clutch a thread hadn't changed since first grade. There is something completely foreign to me about fingering a thin thread. I have no counterpart in my life for such fine motor activity. I've probably avoided every activity with thumb and index finger (except for enforced knitting) since my first-grade encounters with sewing. My whole body toiled. I felt the weight of it in my shoulders, neck, and lower back as those muscular reinforcements poured in to assist their inept cousins in gripping the thin, blue line.

117

I found that remembering the steps for threading the machine was less difficult than mustering the required dexterity. I had Betty do two sequences of about four steps, stop, then pull the thread out from the beginning, so I'd be able to put the successful sequences end to end. This also gave me much-needed practice in holding the thread. I was surprised to find that the sequencing practice had improved my dexterity markedly by the time I had to thread the needle. With only two tries and much wetting of the thread end, I managed it. The bobbin inside the machine took even less time, but I was surprised at my inability to handle cutting the thread on the hook behind the machine. That difficulty came from my own directive stubbornness.

"I've got to see what I'm doing to cut that thread," I barked to Betty. I stood up and leaned over the machine, adjusting my trifocals up and down to see the thread and cutting hook while holding the thread with both hands. I couldn't see the hook and my purchase was poor; the thread wouldn't cut.

"You don't need to see it at all. You have no leverage standing up there, just sit here, reach up behind the machine, and pull on that hook. You don't have to see," she repeated with finality. So much for helping someone teach me. I was dead wrong and had to regroup. I sat as she commanded and easily cut the thread.

The sewing part was easy. I quickly got the feel of the machine, controlling the direction of the cloth, and my raising and lowering the presser foot. Within a few minutes I'd made a small pillow. "Just right for a gerbil," I remarked triumphantly.

BASKETBALL

Betty chose to learn something equally foreign to her. For years she has heard me scream and moan from the next room while I watch the Boston Celtics play basketball on television. "You can teach me about basketball, but I want to interview you before watching any," she said as a condition of agreeing. The following is Betty's fifteen-minute, first-draft account of learning about the game of basketball.

Spectator sports held no interest for me growing up. The men I knew were so busy at farming, teaching, blacksmithing, home repair, radio tinkering, and automobile maintenance, that sports were not important. When there was time for play, they did the playing themselves—ice skating, swimming, sledding, mountain climbing, boating, etc. In my abstemious

New England heritage, none of my forebears would waste money to watch someone else play a sport. Add to the previous attitude my own dislike of beefy men showing off their physical strength and power to push others around, and you have a woman who will find lessons in understanding basketball difficult.

Nevertheless, Don and I sat down at the kitchen table, he with pen and paper to draw diagrams and I with a scheme of questions in my mind that needed consecutive answers. Don drew a three-by-five-inch rectangle for the court with the key and basket markings and put X's and O's for the two teams. Then I started the questioning, controlling the way he filled in the gaps in my information. What are the names of the players' positions? What are the markings on the floor called? What is the task of each player? Tell me about fouls. My questions continued, with Don supplying only the information I asked for. I was enjoying getting the answers just as I need them in the pre-readied slots in my mind.

Eventually we began to discuss the strategies of plays, how the men pass the ball from one to another, how they guard and press. At this point I'm getting confused and can't remember all the details. I ask for repeat information.

Don has a helpful suggestion. "Let's watch the UCLA-Washington State game. It's on TV now." Time to apply my new knowledge.

It is extremely hard for me to interpret all the jangled movement on the screen at one time. I want to know why they call a foul, why the blue team gets possession of the ball. How come the blues score three points for that basket? I am annoyed when my husband discusses the plays with his father and my questions are not immediately answered. I want control.

Don has another helpful suggestion. "Just watch one player."

As I begin to follow number 23 on the blue UCLA team, the game starts to come alive. I feel my first spark of enthusiasm; I can participate in the comments going back and forth between Don and his dad. I am delighted when 23 makes a basket.

In the past my only goal for TV sports events was to get them over as soon as possible, shut the TV off as soon as my husband finished watching it, and return to the normal activities of daily living. On this night I am amazed to hear myself demanding that the men turn the TV back on so I can hear the postgame discussion and learn if 23 was chosen most valuable player for the game. He was not! All I can say is that the officials were not watching 23 as closely as I, and they missed his brilliant strategies.

Learning and teaching "from scratch" are two of the quickest ways I know to gain quick insight into a process. I picked this notion up from Mary Ellen Giacobbe, who was carrying out an assignment while studying at Harvard University. Students worked in pairs alternating as teacher and learner. Mary Ellen took instruction in how to play the piano. In turn, she taught something new to the person who taught her to play. Each kept a detailed journal on their dual roles as teacher and learner.

These examples of learning to use the sewing machine and learning to watch a basketball game, took about half an hour each, and this account is much abbreviated. The principle of observing one player in order to understand a basketball game I transferred to my own professional work. Complex events can be understood better by observing one person. When I do a demonstration with a group of children, I assign one of the children to a team of three teachers, who are to view the entire demonstration through the eyes of that child. Ask one child to take you on a tour of the room and explain how her classroom works.

TRY THIS: Teach someone how to do something he or she knows little about. Reverse the process and learn something you know little about from that person. Write one teaching and one learning story from that practice.

"The Woman in Charge
of Smiles"

I recognized the back of Mother's head above the wheelchair in
the nursing home day room. When I came around to the other
side I found that her eyes were closed. Mother has Alzheimer's
disease. I was visiting the home to report on her condition to
my father, who was in a nearby hospital.

"Mother, this is your son, Donald Hiller Graves," I said in
a loud voice. Her eyelids barely flickered.

A young woman in a white uniform, wearing the lifting
truss of nursing home aides, strode across the room. She
smiled revealing white even teeth beneath large brown eyes.
"Mr. Graves, so good to see you again." "Good" carried a
slight accent.

"Hello, Fatima," I said.

My wife, Betty, spoke her full name. "We remember you,
Mrs. Figueirido."

"Oh, how can you even pronounce my name? How is your
father, Mr. Graves? We miss him." Clearly, she keeps track of
the residents and Dad isn't even on her floor.

Quickly she leaned into Mother's face, no more than six
inches away. "Marion," she said, "How are you?"

Mother opened her eyes, turning her head slowly and deliberately as if guided by an unseen motor. She lifted her face
to Fatima's; a slight smile worked at the corners of her
mouth.

"You know, your father comes down every day and reads
to your mother. I hope my husband does that for me some
day." She pivoted and walked across the room to another
woman in a wheelchair. "Hi Bessie, how are you?" she asked
the upturned face only inches away from a smile.

I think this story is a first cousin to the one about the Australian bus driver. Not unlike our daughter Caroline, Fatima had a way of moving straight to the heart of the matter and applying sudden force. In this case she knew she had to go right "into the face" of residents like my mother, who suffered from senile dementia. She blitzed through the barriers of worn synapses and reached someplace inside that was a source of smiles. How elemental a gift Fatima provided for Mother, for the residents, and especially for us visitors. We were all smiling.

I've seen teachers do the same. Sensing that a child or a student is having a bad day, they move in quickly and, ignoring all possibility of rejection, break through the hard shell of despair.

TRY THIS: Recall someone you know who has a knack for producing smiles where smiles hardly exist. Tell the story. Do you carry that story with you? How do you use it?

The Man on the Plane

When I fly I like to sit on the starboard (right) side in a window seat. I like to look out the window, checking the scene below, cloud conditions, and approaching storms. The starboard side also lets me nap on my right shoulder, my preferred side for sleeping. I always hope the seat to my left will be empty so I can spread out my papers and get some work done.

I was flying from Portland, Maine, to Atlanta, Georgia, and then on to Columbus, Georgia, for a convention address. I was counting on a good stretch of work, as my talk wasn't as well prepared as I'd have liked. Up until the last minute when the cabin doors were secured the seat next to me was empty. I was about to lay out my papers on the seat when a tall, middle-aged man in military fatigues slid into the space. He was about six foot four, lean, with pointed elbows that invaded my arm rest and grazed my side. I could hardly rest my fingers on the computer keys to write.

Since work was out of the question I thought about chatting with my new neighbor. I checked to see what he was reading as the jet took off. It was an article about the Tet Offensive in the *Marine Journal*. I asked him, "Were you there? Were you in Vietnam?"

"Bet your ass," the big man in fatigues answered. "And I want you to know we won that offensive. The press over here made so damn much of our casualties, they never did respect the fact that we beat 'em, beat 'em good. It was horrible though. We lost so many good men. Know what? I couldn't cry then and I can't cry now."

Before I could respond he turned back to his reading. I felt suspended, unsure of what to say. I didn't want the man to think I was indifferent, yet I was without words of assurance.

To let him know I was a friendly guy who didn't want him to feel ignored, I asked, "What has you headed south to Atlanta?"

"My son was killed." He spoke the words with little inflection.

"That's awful. So your son was killed in Georgia? That's why you're flying down to Atlanta?"

"Nah, I'm going down to get my father who can't drive up. See, my son was killed back home. It was a foggy Friday night and he missed a turn on a road he knew and went straight into a tree. His fiancée was riding behind him and saw the whole thing. God, it was awful. Lovely girl, his fiancée. I'm trying to help her all I can. Know what? I still can't cry."

"Where is back home?" I asked. I still didn't know what to say. I just wanted our conversation to keep going and the man seemed to want to talk.

"Boothbay Harbor. Small town on the Maine coast."

"I know that town. How old was your son?"

"Twenty. He was going to school down in Portland. Was going to graduate in the spring."

"Did your son ever have a teacher named Nancie Atwell?"

The big man spun in his seat, his eyes suddenly alive. "You know her? You know this woman?"

"Yes, sir, I do."

"That woman saved my son's life. I mean, he wasn't doing nothin' in school until he got her. She wrote this book and he's got a couple of things in it."

"Yes sir, I know the book. What was your son's name?"

"B. J. Sherman. Yeah, he's got something in there about the time he left his mother and came to live with me. He's got some other things too."

"I remember your son's writing, especially the piece you've just mentioned. It's an honor to meet you, Mr. Sherman." We shook hands.

"They had a funeral for him. All his friends and people from the town came. It was a little country church. You know, so many people came, they couldn't fit 'em all inside. There must have been three hundred people there. I went down to Portland to see his teachers, to tell 'em what happened, and they said he was doing real good in school. Funny, you know, I

124

just wish I could tell B. J. that. But I can't." We continued to talk. Our conversation drifted back to Vietnam and death.

"Mr. Sherman, I'd like to show you something one boy wrote. The boy's name was Sean and he had a teacher, Linda Rief, in the seventh grade who was very much like Nancie Atwell. Like Nancie, she challenged kids to say what was important to them." I reached into my travel bag, took out a copy of *Build a Literate Classroom*, and passed it to him. "This boy struggled like your son, but I think he worked hard to tell the truth." Mr. Sherman picked up the book; his lips moved as he slowly read.

MY DAD IN THE VIETNAM WAR

This story is really hard for me to write. Its about my Dad who was in the Vietnam War. All the terrible things that happened. How he lost really good friends. Or about one day when my Dad was in a Bar. And some kid rolled alive grenade in. It lucky did not exsplode. Or how he would be walking down the street and a Religious monk who had drenched himself with gasoline, would light a match and burn himself to death just because he was protesting. This year at my Dad's birthday, my sister and her friend bought my Dad a book on the Vietnam war. My Dad was happy and sad at the same time. My Dad didn't want to talk about it because he had to maney bad feelings. Someday when my Dad can talk about it. I hope he talks to me.

As Mr. Sherman reached the last line he put his head between his knees and sobbed. I cried right along with him. Two fine boys and two extraordinary teachers brought two strangers together on a flight to Atlanta.

Straight, truthful writing brings people together. (Mr. Sherman and I didn't have a copy of B. J.'s text to discuss, but readers may wish to turn to page 235 in Nancie Atwell's *In the Middle* [1987] to read "Starting Over.") When I got to the airport in Atlanta I immediately called Nancie to tell her about my experience with Mr. Sherman. She said something I've never forgotten: "You know, in B. J.'s case he was struggling to write about leaving his mother as personal narrative. I recommended that he might like to try writing it as fiction. I learned that if you can somehow place writing, or the right genre, between where a person is and where the person wants to go, good things happen."

Good teachers make people want to talk about them, just as I am

Blue Highways and
Red Expressways

I've been running cross-country for thirty-four years, and every once in a while my wife, Betty, accompanies me on her bicycle. When I run alone I punch the timer on my watch, estimate the average time I want for the intervals, especially the hills, and stride forward. Except for checking my watch, my running is a Zen-like activity.

I meditate on different ideas for my writing. During one mile I might consider ideas for speeches and in the next think through a text for Bible study at the church. One of the wonderful things about running is that no telephones or people can suddenly intrude on a good train of thought.

Last October I asked Betty if she'd like to cycle while I ran a five-and-a-half-mile country loop that gradually rises, goes steeply up a mountain, then drops back into town for the last two miles. Out of habit I began my run by thinking about one of the stories for this book. "Is that where the Devellians live?" Betty asked about three hundred yards into the run.

"Yup," I answered. Within a half mile and on the next steep rise she asked another question.

"I wonder if the Eagle Mountain House is making a profit?"

"Suppose so," I answered, reaching for air. On the next downhill incline I commented, "It's hard to talk on the uphill. Maybe you could wait for the next downhill." Betty grunted as if to say, "Then why did you ask me to ride with you while you were running?" She cycled on ahead while I returned to my thoughts. Talking on the uphill doesn't bother me as much as having my thinking interrupted. I checked my watch to see if I was on schedule. The sky was blue, the sun warm, and it was a good day for running.

The next mile and a half were all uphill. I found Betty at the bridge over the Wildcat River staring down into the rushing water. "What a beautiful day!" she exclaimed.

"Yup," I answered, gearing myself for the eight-percent grade of Black Mountain.

When we finally completed the loop and arrived back at the car I remarked, "Great day. Had one of my best times yet."

"Did you see the beaver swimming in the pond at the top of the hill?"

"Uh, no."

"Then I see they are tearing down the house the Historical Society was thinking of buying."

"No kiddin'."

"I thought the view up by those townhouses was so spectacular. You could see all the mountains, the Moats, Attitash, all the way down to Mt. Chocorua. The blue sky and the color of the leaves. Amazing." I hadn't seen a thing, just the grade in the road and the time on my watch.

I run twenty to thirty miles a week, and I wonder how many scenes like these I have missed over the years. I realize how clearly this story typifies the differences between us. Betty takes the blue highways, the country roads that invite her off the main highway in her everyday living. I take the red expressways, planning ahead for what I will write, how I will organize.

Betty is lured by the road not taken. On a car trip, she remarks, "Oh, that looks like an interesting road going up over that hill. Let's take it. We've gone by it many times. Let's have a look."

I groan. "But you know what time we said we'd get there?"

"What difference will it make?"

Or we go to the supermarket. I provide the preprinted list for efficiency. Betty grudgingly takes it but only partially uses it. She ponders some serendipitous new food or fresh produce that is not on the list and later surprises me at the table. She lives in a Technicolor world; mine is black and white.

Any marriage or long-term friendship will produce antithetical stories. This last summer, while preparing a Bible study on the book of Genesis, I ran into an interesting rabbinical translation of the Adam and Eve story. According to my translation, Eve was to be Adam's "helpmate," But the rabbinical scholar in my studies states that "helpmate" should really be translated "antagonist" That is, the helpmate's task is to provide contrast, an edge of difference, that allows both man and woman to reach their full potential as human beings.

I confess that for much of our marriage, many of our small differences have been irritating. Mistakenly I thought, "In a few years she'll change and come around to the obvious ways in which life should be lived." Only recently have I begun to recognize the beauty in the differences.

In 1983 I struggled to write a final report on our study of children's writing for the National Institute of Education. I took the mounds of data we'd collected over two years and I looked for generalizations I could make about writing strategies. I pounded both my head and the table. The data wouldn't give.

I looked out my study window at the home of my neighbor, Jim Pollard. Jim is a pomologist, an expert on fruit trees. I recalled a day when Jim was standing in his yard discussing trees. Though the trees looked the same to me, Jim was fascinated by their differences. He stood there pointing out various patterns of growth, the problems of competitive growth from other trees, incipient diseases he could read in the leaves.

I saw my data in a new light. The point of research is to show differences. Although we deliberately chose children in various categories to represent particular kinds of writers, within a month we were fascinated by their differences.

Like dragons in moonlight no institution spotlights differences better than marriage or the family circle. Differences often upset us. We live as if everyone should be alike. Embrace and celebrate the differences. We shouldn't be surprised to see those dragons.

TRY THIS: Consider someone you have known for a long time. Write or tell a story that reveals the differences between you and the other person.

Walking the Land

Six years ago Betty and I retired to our new home on the side of Iron Mountain in Jackson, New Hampshire. From our front windows we have a full view of snow-capped Mt. Washington just ten miles to the north. The view continues 180 degrees to the south, taking in another eight peaks in the White Mountain range. We've cut trails, thinned timber, and enjoyed the surrounding flora and fauna.

A few weeks ago, 4.4 acres adjacent to and just south of our land were put up for sale. The thought of someone cutting down the birches and hemlocks and constructing a home gave us the shakes. We bought the land. Now we hike it regularly and two days ago hiked it again to rediscover what might be there.

Betty and I hike downhill from the paved town road following an old lane. "Let's bring out that stand of paper birch by cutting down the scrub hemlock that's crowding in," Betty advises.

"I agree. Let's take Peter's advice and cut about every third of the small hemlocks to bring strength to the stand. Take a bit of work. I need to check out the chainsaw to make sure it's ready for next week when we go to town on all of this." A month ago we invited a good friend, Peter Benson, who works for the Nature Conservancy, to do a survey of the new property. We want to be responsible landowners. Although we have title to the land we know that we are only temporary custodians of a sacred trust.

"Do you think the kids would ever want to live here after we're gone?" I ask Betty. "After we're gone" is a phrase that repeats itself with greater frequency these days. Both our mothers passed away within the past four years in their late eighties.

Dad died last January at ninety-three and Betty's father is still living at ninety-seven.

"Heaven only knows where the kids will be by the time we have to give the place up. They all like the outdoors. Some might want to retire here. How long do you figure we have before we have to move to a retirement home?" Betty wonders.

"I figure about fifteen years, maybe when I'm in my mid-eighties. Depends on how much I stay in shape, keep writing, and work the land. Gotta keep movin'. Ideally, I suppose I'd like to make it to ninety before we have to move. Of course, none of this affects how we'll treat the land. Here's the hemlock Peter drilled."

Peter had whipped out a drill that looked like a wine bottle opener from his forester's kit. He turned it corkscrew fashion into one of the larger hemlocks and extracted a thin, cylindrical bore about a quarter-inch in diameter from the inside center to the outside of the tree. We counted the rings and arrived at seventy-five years of age for the tall hemlocks at our lower tree line. We figure our 13.2 acres had last been logged in the early 1920s. We assessed the width of the rings, which showed wet and dry years. Indeed, the core was a virtual weather map of the past seventy-five years.

We move into the tree line and follow the blue dots we've painted for trail markers. The trail takes a diagonal swing against the slope to the bog at the bottom of the hill. Green fern fronds poke through the three-inch snow powder. On top of a granite boulder polypodia rock ferns have found enough soil to take root. "Check this pattern of tracks here," I shout to Betty.

"What do you think, fox or coyote?" We lean down to study the tracks.

"I'd say fox. The paw's too small for a coyote. Foxes are more loners, don't you think? Coyotes travel more together. We'd probably see more than one set of tracks."

"Look where the tracks go," Betty points up the hill. "I'll bet that's the same fox who inspects our frozen garden each night. So what are you going to write after you finish *Shark*?"

"I dunno. I've got a thousand stories left in my head, but there's nothing worse than a storyteller who won't shut up when it's time. I wonder if I'll know when it's time. I think a lot about that."

"You shouldn't be the judge. Write and let the editors decide. They'll tell you the truth."

"Maybe I'm afraid of getting the big No, that indeed it *is* time. Look at this maple bark over here. Fresh deer cut." Deer have only lower teeth and often chew on the bark of trees with an upward thrust of the lower jaw. "Bet they are nipping off the ends of the hobble bush. Yes, look, here are some that are cut off as if you'd taken pruning shears. No blossoms in the spring off this bush."

"Here's where I want to put the bridge next year." I point to two tufted islands about a dozen feet apart. "Next spring we'll put in a ninety-foot log bridge like they do on Nature Conservancy land. Peter said to do it when the water level is highest; then you'll have a dry walkway in the wettest of weather."

Betty adds, "Won't it be nice when we can just stride across and stop slipping on these slimy logs you put in four years ago?" I ponder her words. Yes, we need plans. That's what keeps us moving.

I add, "After we get the bridge in, I'd like to make a blind as an observation post for watching birds and animals." We cross the bog and take another trail parallel to the swampy land.

"There's where the wild azaleas blossom in June and over here the shad. I'd like to find some pitcher plants. They have to be here in a swamp like this." Betty is fascinated by bog flowers or any wildflowers. She's the wildflower expert on our team. Every spring we take to the trails, doing a census of lady slippers, red and painted trilliums, and Indian cucumbers. I record the date of first emergence for each of the wildflowers: star flowers, bunch berries, clintonias, violets, and Indian pipes.

"Look at this. Must have been a snowshoe rabbit convention here." Betty waggles a finger at criss-crossing tracks with the familiar large hind footprints and the two, one, one pattern.

We follow our new-cut trail up the hill to a large glacial erratic boulder about twelve feet long and ten feet high that overlooks the bog. "Now, here's where I want to make a picnic spot." Betty speaks with lowered, serious tones. "Cut out some of the scrub around the boulder. Just look at the range of mosses on it. Green against gray, against the white of snow. Next, we'll cut away a little more and we'll see the whole bog and have a good lookout for raptors that fly over the open spaces."

"Hey, wait a minute," I say. "You've always got me clearing away something. So what year are we going to do that project?" I am trying to tease her a bit, but the look on her face makes me lighten the mood, "Know what? We're playin' house like two little kids."

We decide to leave the main trail and bushwhack diagonally to the back line. We pass through another stand of paper birch. Betty takes her usual side journey while I follow the route we'd planned. I hear a shout off to my right. "Don, come here, quick." She sounds excited, as if she's discovered the den of a hibernating bear. I race over and find her pointing up at a large oak two feet in diameter. It reaches a good seventy feet up to blue sky and white clouds gracefully sailing in from the northwest.

"The way you said 'come here quick,' you'd think that oak was going to run away and disappear," I joke. We stand for nearly five minutes saying nothing, just taking in the oak. "You know, an oak like that has to be at least 150 years old; that's just before the Civil War. We've been hiking out here all this time and we've never seen it."

"Let's clear out around the base and give it some breathing room," Betty advises. "It needs a name like the places we've named on the other lots. You know, like Buffalo Rock and Boulder Park? What about the Generation Tree? It spans the generations."

"Yeah, and it'll be here long after we're gone."

The land is our trust and our teacher. Each hike, whatever the season or the circumstance, provides something new for us to read from the land. Sometimes we carry handbooks to study scat and track, fern, mosses, and wildflowers. There's always more to learn about the trees, especially about how to manage them successfully for maximum growth.

Every season carries its own lessons. I keep a detailed journal recording precipitation, temperature range, and barometric pressure along with a chart on morning sunrise. The mountains to the east allow me to track the sun's rising from near due east in June to the south in early November, ten months out of twelve. With the rhythms of light and season in my bones, each day has its own precious offering.

Our time on earth is short, how short we do not know. I may have only today or I may reach one hundred. I cannot separate learning from living. Indeed, to live is to learn. I pray that I may be open to learning until the last breath of life that is given to me.

TRY THIS: Recall a time when someone taught you something about land that was important to you. Recall a time when you felt in rhythm with the seasons. Recall a time you felt mortal or that the time for living was short, and you made a change in the way you lived your life.